FUNNY VALUES

FUNNY VALUES

by

ROBERT LEACH

W. FOULSHAM & CO. LTD.

London · New York · Toronto · Cape Town · Sydney

W. Foulsham & Company Limited
Yeovil Road, Slough, Berkshire, SL1 4JH

ISBN 0-572-01503-8

Printed in Great Britain by Cox and Wyman Ltd.
Reading.

PREFACE

Did you know that:

- the value wiped off the Stock Exchange on 19 October 1987 would have been sufficient to repay Argentina's national debt?
- the Queen is worth about the same as the Bradford and Bingley Building Society?
- the amount collected annually in road tax is enough to buy a pint of beer for everyone in Asia?
- ICI's profits represent a one-mile-high pile of £20 notes?
- the amount the National Westminster Bank has provided for bad debts from Brazil would pay the UK road repair bill for one year?
- we spend the same on football pools as we do on private health?
- outstanding rents owed to local authorities would buy a Mars bar for everyone in China?
- the amount the UK government lost in abandoning the development of one tank is the same as their spending on the inner cities?
- the value of the consortium owned by disgraced US television evangelist Jim Bakker would pay all the Church of England's clergy for one year?
- the profits of Littlewoods mail order business could fund Cambridge University?
- the amount Barclays Bank spent developing their Connect card is the same as the annual sale of postal orders?
- Madonna earns enough each year to buy 10,000 tons of ice cream?
- UK government expenditure on researching food crops for developing countries is the same as the cost of the two drills for the Channel Tunnel?
- the advertising budget of one unit trust exceeded the annual income of the charity War on Want?
- the amount lost by the *Evening News* in its eight-month reappearance would have paid British Rail's bill for heating railway points?
- the debts written off by Camberwell Health Authority were enough to buy a semi-detached house in Hertfordshire?

- the solicitor-general for Scotland does not earn enough to be classified as a 'top earner' by National and Provincial Building Society?
- Haringey Council paid a heating engineer more than the army pays a major?

All these comparisons, and thousands more, can be made with the aid of this fascinating book, which lists the values and amounts of everything from the sublime to the ridiculous.

You can find out how much your salary is worth. You can find comparisons to justify expenditure of which you approve, and to lampoon expenditure of which you disapprove.

Before You Ask

Unless otherwise stated:
- all figures either refer to the calendar year 1987 or the financial year 1986/87;
- import and export figures refer to 1986;
- prices quoted are those which applied in October 1987;
- where more than one price applied, a typical price has been used;
- distances refer to the shortest route by road (UK) or by air (overseas);
- all sums quoted are in UK sterling;
- investments of a penny quoted are to 1 January 1987.

My thanks go to the Bank of England and many others for their help in providing information.

Although great care has been taken in ensuring the accuracy of the figures included, the author and publisher can accept no responsibility for any inaccuracy contained, for any loss caused by believing that your expenditure was less than the cost of buying everyone in Brazil a Polo mint, or for the loss of friends who get tired of hearing you quote from this book.

Robert Leach, 1988

327,600,000bn	value of 1p invested at 5% in 1066.
92,233,700bn	if you put a penny on the first square of a chess board, 2p on the second square, 4p on the third, 8p on the fourth, and carried on doubling the amount for each subsequent square, this is what you would need for the last square.
62,360,300bn	value of 1p invested at 5% in 1100.
44,843,656bn	what Lake Ontario would be worth if it were full of whisky instead of water.
16,124,534bn	what Lake Ontario would be worth if it were full of 4-star petrol instead of water.
474,218bn	value of 1p invested at 5% in 1200.
3606.18bn	value of 1p invested at 5% in 1300.
2712.5bn	value of a 1,000-mile-high (1,600 km) pile of £50 notes.
1421.9bn	the US gross federal debt at the end of 1986.
700bn	amount wiped off the stock exchanges of London, New York and Tokyo in the first two weeks of the crash of 14–28 October 1987.
677.067bn	the US budget for 1987.
347.6bn	value of property, machinery and cars owned by the UK government (1985).
285bn	debt of Latin-American countries at the end of 1986.
271.25bn	value of a 100-mile-high (160 km) pile of £50 notes.
266bn	money 'lost' in the world's accounts in the first five years of the 1980s. This is the difference between what all the countries say they have borrowed and what they say they have lent.
250bn	estimated total value of all UK pension funds.

222bn	how much the UK government would be worth if it were a limited company.
213.51bn	entire UK household expenditure.
166.65bn	value of a 100-km-high (60 miles) pile of £50 notes.
164.8bn	UK government expenditure for 1986–87.
144.3bn	value of land and buildings owned by the UK government.
127.7bn	value of civil engineering works owned by the UK government.
110bn	Brazil's national debt.
108.91bn	value of a 100-mile-high (160 km) pile of £20 notes.
108bn	cut in the US budget deficit demanded in October.
102bn	Mexico's national debt.
100.8bn	total tax revenue of the UK.
66.7bn	value of a 100-km-high (60 miles) pile of £20 notes.
63bn	value of plant and machinery owned by the UK government.
62.3bn	total expenditure by the Department of Health and Social Security.
59.8bn	value of residential property owned by the UK government.
55.519bn	taxes collected by the Inland Revenue.
54.25bn	value of a 100-mile-high (160 km) pile of £10 notes.
53.7bn	profits of all UK companies.
50bn	Argentina's national debt.

50bn	value wiped off the London Stock Exchange on 19 October 1987.
49.3bn	Brazil's outstanding debts to banks.
48.9bn	Mexico's outstanding debts to banks.
44.5bn	UK imports from the EEC (1986).
44.4bn	expenditure on social security.
43.567bn	Canadian government's income.
43.1bn	total earnings of UK nationalised industries (to 1986).
41.204bn	taxes collected by HM Customs and Excise.
38.499bn	total UK income tax.
38bn	estimated total income of the top 5% of tax-payers.
37.9bn	amount given by central government to local authorities.
35bn	UK exports to the EEC (1986).
33.33bn	value of a 100-km-high (60 miles) pile of £10 notes.
30bn	value wiped off the London Stock Exchange in the first few hours of 26 October 1987.
28.694bn	assets of the Halifax Building Society (the largest).
28bn	estimated proceeds from privatising the electricity industry.
27.538bn	limit on local authority spending for 1988/89.
27.4232bn	value of 1p invested at 5% in 1400.
27.125bn	value of a 100-mile-high (160 km) pile of £5 notes.
25.3bn	total outstanding amount of consumer credit (April).

23.837bn	total national insurance collected.
23.041bn	assets of the Abbey National Building Society.
23bn	how much tourism will be worth to the UK in 1990.
21.4228bn	total value added tax collected.
20.8bn	Argentina's outstanding debts to banks.
18.5bn	Venezuela's outstanding debts to banks.
18.287bn	assets of the Nationwide Anglia Building Society.
18.149bn	UK government expenditure on defence.
17.9bn	expenditure by the DHSS on health and personal services.
17.6bn	annual interest on the UK government debt.
17.14bn	Unilever's turnover.
17bn	value wiped off shares in the 'three-day tumble' in August 1987.
16.5bn	value of a 100-km-high (60 miles) pile of £5 notes.
15.8bn	annual UK expenditure on alcoholic drink.
15.7bn	annual cost of the Department of Education and Science.
15bn	estimated wealth of the Sultan of Brunei (world's richest person).
14.1bn	UK imports from Germany.
13.495bn	total corporation tax.
13.4bn	amount lent by members of the Finance Houses Association.
12.8bn	value of pension funds managed by Mercury Warburg Investment Management (largest fund managers).

12.754bn	Canada's budget deficit.
12.6bn	total given to charity from UK populace.
12bn	estimated wealth of King Fahd of Saudi Arabia.
11.5bn	extra tax bill if Labour won the general election (according to Norman Tebbit).
11.2bn	tax liability of the wealthiest 5% of the population of the UK.
10.89bn	value of a 10-mile-high (16 km) pile of £20 notes.
10.7bn	UK imports from the Benelux states.
10.38bn	UK exports to the USA.
10.072bn	UK trade deficit with the EEC.
9.7bn	Philippines' outstanding debt to the world's banks.
9.584bn	assets of the Woolwich Building Society.
9.4bn	amount spent on meals out in the UK.
9.3bn	UK exports to the Benelux states.
9.265bn	cost of the Trident nuclear missile programme.
8.8bn	value of pension funds managed by Robert Fleming Investment Management.
8.7bn	Chile's outstanding debt to the world's banks.
8.5bn	UK exports to Germany.
8.47bn	UK imports from the USA.
8.4bn	profits from North Sea oil.
8.094bn	annual equipment cost for the Ministry of Defence.
8.101bn	assets of the Alliance and Leicester Building Society.

8bn	annual lending by the World Bank.
8bn	value added to the London Stock Market on the day after the Conservatives won the 1987 general election.
7.97bn	value of worldwide sales of telecommunications equipment.
7.8bn	value of pension funds managed by Schroder Investment Managers.
7.7bn	annual cost of the Scottish Office.
7.5076bn	total collected as hydrocarbon oil duty.
7.492bn	value of pension funds managed by Phillips and Drew Fund Management.
7.3bn	UK imports from France.
7.2bn	value of BP shares floated in October.
7.1bn	annual expenditure by local authorities (gross).
6.9bn	amount lent to businesses by members of the Finance Houses Association.
6.667bn	value of a 10-km-high (6 miles) pile of £20 notes.
6.606bn	annual wage bill for the Ministry of Defence.
6.5bn	total expenditure by the Department of the Environment.
6.5bn	amount lent to consumers by members of the Finance Houses Association.
6.396bn	purchases made using an Access card.
6.2bn	UK exports to France.
6.165bn	value of pension funds managed by County Investment Management.
6.048bn	assets of the National and Provincial Building Society.

6bn	tax revenues from alcoholic drink.
6bn	expenditure on the elderly, mentally ill and handicapped.
6bn	estimated cost of the Channel Tunnel.
6bn	amount in dispute between Texaco and Pennzoil in the USA.
5.8bn	annual cost of the Home Office.
5.6bn	amount spent in the UK by tourists.
5.582bn	UK trade deficit in 1986.
5.5bn	value of vehicles owned by the UK government.
5.42bn	value of a 10-mile-high (16 km) pile of £10 notes.
5.391bn	purchases made using a Barclaycard.
5.3bn	estimated wealth of Sam Moore Walton, owner of Wal-Mart discount stores.
5.2bn	industrial investment funded by leasing.
4.932bn	UK imports from Japan.
4.9bn	bank lending in July (record).
4.8bn	value of securities traded every day on the London Stock Exchange.
4.7676bn	total collected in excise duty on tobacco.
4.741bn	UK exports of aerospace products.
4.7bn	UK imports from Italy.
4.7bn	annual cost of the Department of Transport.
4.6bn	annual cost of the Northern Ireland Office.
4.574bn	annual wage bill for the armed forces.
4.5bn	estimated wealth of the Queen.
4.417bn	assets of the Bradford and Bingley Building Society.

4.4bn	proceeds of privatisation.
4.4bn	consumer borrowing in September.
4.353bn	cost of buying a pint of beer for everyone in the world.
4.3bn	Brazil's outstanding debt to the Midland Bank.
4.3bn	Brazil's outstanding debt to Lloyds Bank.
4.3bn	Colombia's outstanding debt to the world's banks.
4.3bn	Peru's outstanding debt to the world's banks.
4.212bn	assets of the Britannia Building Society.
4bn	agricultural property owned by the UK government.
3.9bn	annual cost of the Department of Employment.
3.854bn	assets of the Cheltenham and Gloucester Building Society.
3.8bn	pre-tax profits of the UK clearing banks.
3.8bn	annual cost of road accidents in the UK.
3.7bn	total amount spent on furniture in 1986.
3.7bn	annual expenditure by local authorities (net).
3.6bn	UK exports to the Republic of Ireland.
3.527bn	value of pension funds managed by Baring Investment Management
3.47bn	UK exports to Italy.
3.41bn	value of shares owned by unit trusts.
3.4bn	estimated cost to business of alcoholism and drug abuse.
3.357bn	loss in value of BP shares in the first week after their flotation.

3.333bn	value of a 10-km-high (6 miles) pile of £10 notes.
3.3bn	value of purchases made by mail order.
3.265bn	UK imports from Norway.
3.207bn	amount spent on sports equipment.
3.2bn	UK consumer credit in March (record).
3.132bn	value of pension funds managed by Lloyds Investment Managers.
3.1bn	annual cost of the Welsh Office.
3.1bn	Brazil's outstanding debt to Barclays Bank.
3.065bn	value of pension funds managed by Henderson Pension Funds Management.
3.05bn	UK imports from Italy.
3.032bn	total cost of programmes run by the Manpower Services Commission.
3.008bn	value of pension funds managed by Kleinwort Grieveson Investment Management.
3bn	value of one order from Saudi Arabia for military aircraft.
3bn	value of docklands development at Canary Wharf, London.
2.989bn	UK imports from Switzerland.
2.98bn	value of pension funds managed by N.M. Rothschild Asset Management.
2.95bn	UK consumer credit for February (record).
2.85bn	amount spent buying chocolate.
2.8bn	estimated cost to the taxpayer of all road accidents.
2.772bn	BP's exports.
2.771bn	ICI's exports.

2.756bn	UK imports from Sweden.
2.716bn	amount wiped off the value of ICI's shares in the first week of the stock market crash of October 1987.
2.71bn	value of a 10-mile-high (16 km) pile of £5 notes.
2.7bn	public offer for Rolls-Royce shares.
2.66bn	amount wiped off the value of BAT's shares in the first week of the stock market crash of October 1987.
2.6bn	Department of the Environment's expenditure on housing.
2.576bn	amount collected in motor vehicle excise duty.
2.531bn	cost of buying a pint of beer for everyone in Asia.
2.514bn	tourist expenditure in the first six months of 1987.
2.5bn	projected expenditure on improving pubs in the next three years.
2.5bn	annual value of unit-linked pension mortgages.
2.452bn	amount wiped off the value of Shell's shares in the first week of the stock market crash of October 1987.
2.4bn	estimated wealth of the Duke of Westminster.
2.4bn	tax on sport.
2.31bn	UK exports to Sweden.
2.3bn	annual cost of the Department of Trade and Industry.
2.3bn	sales by GUS, the country's largest mail order company.

2.3bn	daily amount traded on the London Stock Exchange in August.
2.19bn	investment assets of the Church of England.
2.1bn	annual expenditure of the Lord Chancellor's departments.
2.0714bn	British Aerospace's exports.
2.067bn	British Telecom's profits.
2bn	estimated amount of cash stored 'under the mattress' in the UK.
2bn	estimated annual cost of alcoholism at work.
1.996bn	annual wage cost for civilians working in the Ministry of Defence.
1.986bn	cost of drugs used by the National Health Service.
1.98bn	amount wiped off the value of British Telecom's shares in the first week of the stock market crash of October 1987.
1.958bn	Shell's exports.
1.9742bn	amount the state collects in excise duty from beer.
1.926bn	annual cost of the Foreign Office.
1.9bn	UK exports to Spain.
1.9bn	value of pension funds managed by MIM.
1.8601bn	total collected in stamp duty.
1.847bn	value of pension funds managed by Fidelity International Investment Advisors (UK).
1.838bn	amount wiped off the value of Cable and Wireless's shares in the first week of the stock market crash of October 1987.
1.8bn	annual cost of the Ministry of Agriculture, Fisheries and Food.

1.8bn	amount shareholders in British Gas had to pay on the second instalment of their shares.
1.777bn	UK imports from Spain.
1.754bn	value of pension funds managed by Hambros Bank.
1.752bn	UK imports from Denmark.
1.72bn	value of Toshiba products sold in the USA.
1.715bn	amount spent on office refurbishment.
1.7bn	Brazil's outstanding debt to the Standard Chartered Bank.
1.7bn	value of pension funds managed by Murray Johnstone Pension Management.
1.698bn	UK exports to Canada.
1.674bn	value of pension funds managed by Cazenove.
1.665bn	value of a 10-km-high (6 miles) pile of £5 notes.
1.62bn	amount shareholders in British Gas had to pay on the third and final instalment on their shares.
1.604bn	money exchanged for chips in British casinos in 1986.
1.576bn	value of pension funds managed by Lazards Investors.
1.575bn	UK exports to Switzerland.
1.53bn	UK imports from Hong Kong.
1.507bn	UK exports to Saudi Arabia.
1.5bn	balance written off by Citicorp for Third World debt.
1.5bn	UK imports from Canada.
1.5bn	UK government's 'financial support' to farmers.

1.5bn	estimated wealth of John Moores of Littlewoods.
1.5bn	UK family donations to charity.
1.5bn	state subsidy of the coal industry.
1.4692bn	amount the state collects in excise duty on spirits.
1.432bn	IBM's exports.
1.4bn	estimated cost to business of drug abuse.
1.4bn	pension funds managed by Charterhouse Investment Management.
1.35bn	UK imports from Finland.
1.305bn	UK government's budget for overseas aid.
1.3045bn	total amount collected in customs duties.
1.3bn	estimated wealth of Rupert Murdoch.
1.3bn	state aid given to industry in the last 14 years.
1.3bn	amount Glasgow District Council believe it will cost to bring their housing stock up to standard.
1.292bn	amount wiped off the value of RTZ's shares in the first week of the stock market crash of October 1987.
1.292bn	value of pension funds managed by Legal and General Investment Management.
1.276bn	GEC's exports.
1.245bn	latest estimate of the cost of building Sizewell B nuclear power station.
1.23bn	UK exports to Australia.
1.211bn	UK exports to Denmark.
1.21bn	sale of unit trusts in March (record).
1.21bn	value of UK company buy-outs.

1.2bn	amount spent on kitchen storage units in 1986.
1.2bn	the size of the Roman Catholic Church's agricultural fund to inject western capital into Poland's shareholdings.
1.2bn	daily amount traded in 'domestic equities' in August.
1.194bn	UK exports to Japan.
1.188bn	amount collected in petrol revenue tax.
1.148bn	UK exports to Norway.
1.14bn	Unilever's profits.
1.134bn	annual cost of Inland Revenue.
1.1152bn	Esso's exports.
1.102bn	amount wiped off the value of the National Westminster Bank's shares in the first week of the stock market crash of October 1987.
1.064bn	total collected in capital gains tax.
1.0537bn	what a double decker bus would be worth if it was made of gold.
1.1bn	UK annual net contribution to the EEC.
1.1bn	value of pension funds managed by Touche Remnant Pension Funds Management.
1.1bn	value of UK diesel engine industry.
1.09bn	Ford Motor Company's exports.
1.089bn	value of a 1-mile-high (1.6 km) pile of £20 notes.
1.061bn	ICI's profits.
1.032bn	profits of all building societies.
1.0262bn	annual cost of repairing UK roads.
1.025bn	amount wiped off the value of Beecham's

shares in the first week of the stock market crash of October 1987.

1bn   amount spent on upholstery in 1986.

1bn   Lloyds Bank's provision for Brazil's bad debts.

1bn   value of pension funds managed by Geoffrey Morley and Partners.

1bn   the Church of England's investment in commercial and residential property.

1bn   amount of gilts floated in the first such auction (in May).

999,000,000   British Steel's exports.

995,000,000   estimated finance limits imposed on the nationalised industries.

995,000,000   total collected in inheritance tax.

967,500,014   cost of buying everyone in the world a Mars bar.

960,596,000   UK exports to Hong Kong.

960,400,000   total collected in vehicle excise duty (road tax).

953,568,875   cost of buying a pint of beer for everyone in China.

941,169,000   UK exports to India.

934,000,000   amount wiped off the value of GEC's shares in the first week of the stock market crash of October 1987.

918,000,000   Rolls-Royce's exports.

916,000,000   the Midland Bank's provisions for bad debts from Brazil.

900,000,000   amount spent on beds and bedroom furniture in 1986.

900,000,000	value of offer for sale of British Airways' shares.
895,000,000	profits of Barclays Bank.
871,000,000	debts of Manchester Council (end of 1986).
867,000,000	Third World debt written off by Chase Manhattan Bank.
860,000,000	amount wiped off the value of Reed International's shares in the first week of the stock market crash of October 1987.
850,000,000	personal wealth of Mr Garfield, supermarket owner.
849,557,000	UK exports to South Africa.
837,000,000	record rights issue (Blue Arrow in May).
830,000,000	cost of programme announced by British Rail to relieve overcrowding in trains, particularly in the south east.
829,305,000	UK imports from South Africa.
828,000,000	the National Westminster Bank's provision for bad debts from Brazil.
826,300,000	cost of repairing roads in England.
812,000,000	amount wiped off the value of News International's shares in the first week of the stock market crash of October 1987.
800,000,000	annual expenditure of the Department of Arts and Libraries.
790,000,000	amount lost by the underwriters of the BP flotation.
781,700,000	UK government receipts in betting and gaming duty.
779,000,000	turnover of Littlewoods mail order business.
777,000,000	what the TSB paid to buy Hill Samuel.

772,129,000	value of £10 notes placed end to end from London to Sydney.
768,470,000	UK imports from Portugal.
768,000,000	Rover's exports.
760,000,000	Blue Arrow's bid for Manpower.
750,000,000	cost of developing the new Airbus.
747,000,000	UK exports of machine tools.
738,800,000	estimated wealth of David Sainsbury.
735,000,000	annual budget of the Housing Corporation.
714,000,000	Public Service Obligation payment by the government to British Rail.
712,000,000	Glaxo's liquid funds.
705,775,000	UK imports from Taiwan.
705,732,000	UK imports from Austria.
700,000,000	management buy-out of MFI and Hygena (October).
698,500,000	amount collected in excise duty on wine.
694,624,000	UK imports from the USSR.
680,000,000	losses caused by the PCW fraud at Lloyd's.
680,000,000	extra UK government funds provided to continue bailing out the Rover group.
675,809,982	cost of buying a pint of beer for everyone in India.
666,700,000	value of a 1-km-high (0.6 mile) pile of £20 notes.
664,461,000	UK exports to Finland.
663,600,000	salaries paid to Inland Revenue staff.
661,975,000	UK imports from South Korea.
650,000,000	amount British Road Federation want to see spent on improving roads.

645,000,000	what Ladbroke paid for Hilton.
643,238,000	UK imports from Australia.
635,000,000	sales of machine tools made in the UK.
631,000,000	annual 'diplomatic, information and cultural' expenditure by the Foreign Office.
620,000,000	Jaguar's exports.
610,000,000	Christian Dior's turnover, excluding cosmetics and perfume.
600,000,000	estimated profits made in a racket selling faked Salvador Dali prints.
600,000,000	turnover of the private health sector.
600,000,000	estimated wealth of Sir James Goldsmith.
600,000,000	amount spent each year on furniture and shelving.
598,603,000	amount staked in the football pools.
581,762,000	UK exports to the United Arab Emirates.
570,000,000	Barclays Bank's provision for Brazil's bad debts.
566,176,000	UK exports to Nigeria.
562,600,008	cost of buying a Mars bar for everyone living in China.
560,800,000	National Savings receipts in January (record).
552,259,000	UK imports from Brazil.
550,000,000	estimated amount of assets sold by eight London boroughs in their 'creative accounting'.
550,000,000	average monthly income of the UK building societies for the first six months of 1987.
547,419,000	UK exports to Singapore.
546,000,000	amount the UK government 'bargained off' the Trident programme.

542,540,000	value of a 1-mile-high (1.6 km) pile of £10 notes.
539,368,000	UK exports to the USSR.
537,000,000	amount by which local authorities underspent the rent budget set by the UK Government.
535,943,000	UK exports to China.
502,700,000	estimated wealth of Robert Maxwell.
500,000,000	estimated annual savings made in the National Health Service under the government's cost improvement programmes.
500,000,000	an (unproven) estimate made of the extra amount made by British Telecom from wrong meter readings.
500,000,000	amount local authorities would save if they used private contractors fully (per Audit Commission).
495,000,000	the National Westminster Bank's provision for unpaid debts from Brazil.
492,102,600	value of £10 notes laid end to end from London to Singapore.
487,000,000	amount Rupert Murdoch's shares went down in value in the first week of the stock market crash of October 1987.
487,000,000	Britoil's exports.
484,000,000	the UK government's expenditure on bilateral aid.
480,700,000	amount London University raised by selling courses.
480,000,000	amount need to improve the roads in Surrey, according to the British Road Federation.
472,078,000	UK exports to Portugal.
470,900,000	Texaco's exports.

469,000,000	Jaguar's turnover.
465,000,000	amount of diesel excess duty paid by UK hauliers above what their European counterparts would have to pay for the same amount of diesel.
462,878,000	UK imports from Singapore.
462,407,000	UK exports to Israel.
455,694,000	UK imports from New Zealand.
455,500,000	insurance claims for loss by fire.
450,000,000	amount spent on furniture and shelving in 1985.
449,976,000	amount staked on Littlewoods football pools.
448,000,000	UK imports of sports equipment.
443,890,000	UK exports to Iraq.
445,181,200	value of £10 notes placed end to end from London to Tokyo.
440,681,000	UK imports from India.
435,930,000	UK imports from Saudi Arabia.
435,000,000	annual cost of defending the Falkland Islands.
434,000,000	profits of the Midland Bank.
433,753,000	UK exports to Turkey.
433,000,000	Conoco's exports.
418,000,000	BAT Industries' exports.
412,000,000	Unilever's exports.
406,605,000	UK imports from Turkey.
404,400,000	amount spent on telecommunications equipment.
404,000,000	Courtauld's exports.
403,000,000	UK exports to Austria.

402,200,000	amount of tax recovered by the Inland Revenue from its investigation work.
400,000,000	provision made by the Standard Chartered Bank against unpaid debts from Brazil.
400,000,000	amount claimed by Britons against pre-1917 Russian bonds.
399,647,000	UK exports to Oman.
399,373,000	UK exports to Iran.
396,400,100	value of £10 notes placed end to end from London to Mexico City.
393,000,000	Glaxo's exports.
391,000,000	duty collected on imported cigarettes.
388,000,000	annual expenditure by the Foreign Office on overseas representation.
385,164,000	UK imports from Israel.
384,000,000	Mobil Oil's exports.
383,811,400	value of £10 notes placed end to end from London to San Francisco.
381,000,000	imports of machine tools.
377,400,000	Guinness's exports.
375,200,000	amount paid out by UK insurance companies.
372,000,000	Department of Trade and Industry expenditure on civil industrial research.
371,007,000	UK exports to Egypt.
370,000,000	estimated cost to the National Health Service of dealing with smoking-related illnesses.
364,499,990	cost of buying a pint of beer for everyone in Latin America.
362,000,000	British Gas's profit.
359,000,000	amount paid by WPP for JWT, the Madison Avenue advertising group.

358,000,000	Johnson Matthey's exports.
356,700,000	Kodak's exports.
356,020,000	UK exports to Greece.
350,058,000	UK imports from Malaysia.
350,000,000	estimated wealth of the Vatican, excluding art treasures.
346,800,000	Australia's trade deficit.
343,145,000	UK exports to New Zealand.
342,400,000	estimated wealth of Alan Sugar, chairman of Amstrad plc (February).
340,640,000	price of 100,000 tons of mint imperials.
337,000,000	Philips Industries' exports.
333,300,000	value of a 1-km-high (0.6 mile) pile of £10 notes.
330,000,000	estimated cost to insurance companies of the harsh winter of January 1987.
329,036,000	UK imports from Nigeria.
328,053,000	UK imports from Egypt.
327,032,000	UK imports from China.
325,000,000	amount spent on paint.
323,500,000	rights issue from Norsk Hydro.
315,000,000	NEI's exports.
313,600,000	price of 100,000 tons of Liquorice Allsorts.
309,746,000	UK imports from Poland.
308,644,000	UK imports from Greece.
306,000,000	estimated proceeds from privatising the National Bus Company.
305,860,400	value of £1 coins placed edge to edge from London to Sydney.

305,000,000	amount lent by the government of Hong Kong to its stock exchange to prevent the collapse of the financial futures market in the October 1987 stock market crash.
304,640,000	price of 100,000 tons of Turkish delight.
300,586,000	UK exports to Kuwait.
300,000,000	estimated insurance claims from the October hurricane.
300,000,000	value of books and records stolen from Lambeth Council in 12 months. Many were found on sale on local market stalls.
297,700,000	profit from GUS, the UK's largest mail order business.
295,152,000	UK exports to Brazil.
288,421,000	UK exports to South Korea.
283,000,000	Rolls-Royce's debts written off by the UK government.
279,000,000	STC's exports.
276,000,000	Rothman's exports.
274,000,000	BTR's exports.
273,100,000	Rank Xerox's exports.
271,270,000	value of a 1-mile-high (1.6 km) pile of £5 notes.
270,000,000	cost of British Gas's dividend on shares.
269,000,000	exports of UK-made machine tools.
268,000,000	UK government grants to charities.
267,700,000	road repair bill for south-east England.
267,000,000	BICC's exports.
262,000,000	amount which Procter and Gamble wrote off in its accounts following a 'restructuring'.

260,529,000	UK exports to Libya.
259,500,000	Racal's exports.
258,400,000	price of 100,000 tons of chocolate.
254,406,000	tax on football pools.
250,905,593	cost of buying a pint of beer for everyone in the USSR.
250,000,000	amount paid by United Newspapers to buy Extel.
250,000,000	EEC agricultural levies collected by the UK government.
249,900,000	insurance claims for stolen goods.
238,800,000	UK government grant to London University.
238,400,000	Esso Chemical's exports.
227,064,000	UK exports to Pakistan.
226,912,000	UK exports to Malaysia.
225,000,000	estimated saving in the Ministry of Defence's annual energy bill after an efficiency drive.
225,000,000	cost of the British Gas share flotation, which was criticised by the National Audit Office.
225,000,000	value of electrical goods sold by Thorn-EMI.
218,000,000	expenditure on the first phase of the British Library near St Pancras.
216,700,000	Beecham's exports.
211,904,203	cost of buying a Mars bar for everyone living in China.
211,000,000	overdue rents not collected by local authorities.
210,000,000	capital raised by Barclays Bank in a share issue in New York and Tokyo.
210,000,000	pension funds' investments in unquoted companies.

208,539,000	value of 1p invested at 5% in 1500.
208,000,000	rights issue from Argyll.
207,200,000	fees earned by accounting firms Peat Marwick and KMG to 1987 (when they merged).
207,000,000	UK exports of sports equipment.
205,000,000	Turner Newell's exports.
204,900,000	wealth of Asil Nadir, of Polly Peck.
203,400,000	payments by ITV companies to Channel 4 and Welsh Channel 4.
201,499,000	amount of property 'sold' by Manchester Council as part of a creative accounting package to beat government limits.
200,000,000	estimated value of treasure on the ship *Medina*, found sunk off the Devon coast. It was sunk in 1917.
200,000,000	estimated annual saving on motorway maintenance by replacing tarmacadam with a new concrete.
200,000,000	Malcolm Healey's gain on selling Hygena to MFI.
200,000,000	assets sold by Merton Council to raise funds for it to invest in the stock market.
200,000,000	estimated amount wasted each year from poor purchasing policy of the UK water authorities.
197,000,000	UK government's bilateral aid to sub-Saharan Africa.
196,629,000	UK exports to Indonesia.
196,400,000	the Wellcome Foundation's exports.
195,839,700	value of £10 notes placed end to end from London to Tehran.
195,513,000	UK imports from East Germany.

195,000,000	UK government's bilateral aid to South and East Asia.
192,492,000	UK exports to Taiwan.
190,000,000	value wiped off Ladbroke Group's shares in two days on the basis of a rumour of damaging allegations to be published in a Sunday newspaper.
190,000,000	amount for which the UK government sold the Royal Ordnance munitions business to British Aerospace.
188,390,000	UK exports to Yugoslavia.
187,259,896	cost of buying a pint of beer for everyone in the USA.
185,000,000	incentives (mainly discounts) offered in share flotation of British Gas. They were criticised by the National Audit Office.
183,000,000	Pearson's exports.
182,852,000	UK imports from the Philippines.
182,841,000	UK exports to Poland.
182,400,000	Babcock's exports.
182,756,000	UK imports from Thailand.
178,000,000	extra cost from abolishing the GLC, according to the Association of Local Authorities.
176,347,900	value of £1 coins placed edge to edge from London to Tokyo.
175,000,000	amount spent each year on wallpaper and other wall coverings.
173,140,000	UK imports from Iceland.
173,000,000	British Coal's exports.
170,671,000	UK exports to Kenya.
170,101,000	UK exports to Venezuela.

166,700,000	value of 1-km-high (0.6 mile) pile of £5 notes.
165,500,000	amount lost by Volkswagen in fraudulent currency dealing by an employee.
163,745,000	UK imports from Kenya.
163,400,000	ITV companies' contributions to Channel 4.
163,400,000	Gulf Oil's exports.
162,328,000	UK exports to Mexico.
162,100,000	loss made by the Rover Group.
161,900,000	Plessey's exports.
160,000,000	value of the Duke of Northumberland's 100,000-acre estate.
160,000,000	cost of British Telecom's plans to modernise telephone boxes.
159,000,000	fines and fees collected by the UK courts.
158,195,000	UK exports to Thailand.
157,024,400	value of £1 coins placed edge to edge from London to Mexico City.
154,146,000	UK exports to Brunei.
153,271,000	UK imports from Mauritius.
150,800,000	Church of England's income.
150,300,000	cost of Enterprise Allowance scheme.
150,180,002	cost of buying a Mars bar for everyone living in India.
150,000,000	Spitalfields Development Group's offer for the Spitalfields market site.
148,526,996	cost of buying a pint of beer for everyone in Indonesia.
147,400,000	Short Brothers' exports.
146,800,000	fees earned by accountants Peat Marwick and Mitchell.

145,127,000	UK imports from Yugoslavia.
143,000,000	fees earned by accountants Coopers and Lybrand in the year to 31 March 1987.
143,000,000	price paid for Bracken House, the old *Financial Times* building.
142,600,000	Associated Octel's exports.
141,473,684	UK street value of 1 ton of heroin.
141,242,000	UK imports from Indonesia.
140,860,000	UK imports from Algeria.
140,700,000	amount spent buying PABX telephone switchboards.
140,387,000	UK exports to Cyprus.
140,100,000	price of 100,000 tons of ice cream.
139,600,000	fees earned by accountants Price Waterhouse.
136,390,000	UK imports from Libya.
134,400,000	value of Caradon, the bathroom specialist company, when floated.
134,000,000	value of the rescue package announced by Lloyd's to compensate members who lost money in the PCW fraud.
132,700,000	annual road repair bill in Scotland.
131,296,000	UK imports from Pakistan.
130,991,000	UK exports to Bahrain.
130,700,000	Cadbury Schweppes' profit.
130,385,000	UK exports to Jordan.
130,000,000	value of Haringey Council's pension fund.
129,624,000	UK exports to Algeria.
129,200,000	estimated wealth of Tiny Rowland, chairman of the Lonrho Group.

128,007,000	UK imports from Chile.
127,374,000	tax paid by Vernons Pools.
127,080,000	value of a 2,500-ft-high (762 m) pile of £5 notes.
125,800,000	Monsanto's exports.
125,399,000	UK imports from Czechoslovakia.
125,100,000	value of shares owned by Richard Branson (February).
124,198,000	UK imports from Cyprus.
122,200,000	turnover of Lloyd's.
121,900,000	British Nuclear Fuels' exports.
121,100,000	fees earned by accountants Deloitte Haskins and Sells.
120,000,000	paid by Warners Bros to buy Chappel & Co, music publishers.
120,000,000	Rolls-Royces' profits.
119,000,000	Westland Helicopters' exports.
118,200,000	Michelin Tyres' exports.
118,000,000	amount spent by public visiting historic homes.
118,000,000	amount spent buying wall tiles.
117,058,000	UK imports from the Ivory Coast.
116,078,000	UK imports from Mexico.
115,300,000	Woolworths' profits.
114,600,000	Smiths Industries' exports.
113,218,000	UK exports to Ghana.
112,143,000	UK exports to Qatar.
112,000,000	value of mushrooms eaten in Britain in 1986.
111,700,000	Ingersoll Rand's exports.

111,000,000	UK government expenditure on the countryside and recreation bodies.
110,700,000	Pilkington Brothers' (glass makers) exports.
109,565,997	cost of buying a pint of beer for everyone in Japan.
108,841,000	UK exports to Czechoslovakia.
108,800,000	Dowty's exports.
108,600,000	income generated by the English Tourist Board from £14 million invested in 630 projects.
108,400,000	road repair bill in south-west England.
107,300,000	Pirelli's exports.
106,952,000	value of 1,000 tons of £1 coins.
106,000,000	Marks and Spencer's exports.
104,000,000	UK government grants to the BBC for the External Service.
103,600,000	saving from abolishing the GLC and the metropolitan councils (government figures).
103,480,000	UK imports from Ghana.
103,000,000	Reed Industries' exports.
101,877,000	UK exports to Malta.
101,557,000	UK exports to Hungary.
101,400,000	turnover of EMAP, newspaper publishers.
101,000,000	Foreign Office annual expenditure on broadcasting.
100,700,000	fees earned by accountants Ernst and Whinney in the year to 31 March 1987.
100,303,000	UK imports from Iran.
100,000,000	amount the Post Office intends to start spending from late 1988 to cut down queues at post offices.

$\mathcal{L}$

100,000,000	amount needed to improve the M25 in Surrey in the next ten years, according to the British Road Federation.
100,000,000	amount wasted on road improvements because of non-cooperation between local authorities, according to the Audit Commission.
100,000,000	amount spent on Easter eggs.
99,800,000	amount spent buying telephones.
99,400,000	road repair bill for north-west England.
97,920,680	value of £1 coins placed edge to edge from London to New York.
97,700,000	amount Oxford University earns from selling courses.
97,000,000	amount spent on skiing holidays.
96,400,000	UK government estimate of saving from abolishing the GLC.
96,339,000	UK imports from Venezuela.
96,000,000	May and Baker's exports.
95,816,000	UK exports to the Bahamas.
94,112,000	UK imports from Colombia.
93,600,000	fees earned by accountants Touche Ross.
93,500,000	road repair bill for Yorkshire and Humberside.
93,400,000	Cookson Group's exports.
91,300,000	fees earned by accountants Arthur Andersen.
90,600,000	Tesco's profits.
90,200,000	British Shipbuilders' profits.
90,000,000	fees earned by accountants Arthur Young.
90,000,000	amount spent on electrical DIY equipment.

89,000,000	government expenditure on inner cities.
88,000,000	cost of the tank abandoned by the UK government; the SP-70 howitzer.
87,500,000	Goodyear Tyres' exports.
87,416,000	UK imports from Jamaica.
87,236,000	UK imports from Oman.
86,900,000	Allied Lyons' exports.
86,730,000	UK imports from Romania.
86,000,000	value of PTL, the US gospel consortium run by the now disgraced television evangelist Jim Bakker.
85,800,000	total cost of all Church of England clergy stipends.
85,400,000	turnover of Addison Consultancy, the largest design consultancy.
85,300,000	Cadbury Schweppes' exports.
84,700,000	amount Cambridge University earned from selling courses.
84,510,000	UK exports to Morocco.
83,335,000	UK exports to Sudan.
83,316,000	UK exports to Sri Lanka.
82,300,000	Fison's exports.
82,141,000	UK imports from Peru.
82,011,000	UK exports to Romania.
81,500,000	Boots' exports.
81,284,000	value of 2,000 tons of 20p coins.
81,276,000	UK exports to East Germany.
81,131,000	UK imports from Puerto Rico.
81,000,000	cost of buying a Mars bar for everyone living in Latin America.

80,900,000	London and Scottish Marine Oil Company's exports.
80,702,000	UK imports from Zimbabwe.
80,518,311	what one second's flow over the Niagara Falls would be worth if it were champagne rather than water.
80,504,000	UK exports to Bulgaria.
80,000,000	UK government investment in Midlands' airports since 1979.
80,000,000	amount spent on research by the world's oil companies.
79,900,000	cost of proposed coal pit at Margam, held up in trade union wrangling over working hours.
79,809,000	UK exports to Philippines.
79,029,000	UK exports to Trinidad and Tobago.
78,509,000	UK imports from Curaçao.
78,380,000	UK government funding for derelict land reclamation.
78,000,000	insurance claims for damage to commercial premises.
77,840,000	UK exports to Zambia.
77,577,200	value of £1 coins placed edge to edge from London to Tehran.
77,400,000	road repair bill for the West Midlands.
77,228,000	UK imports from Hungary.
77,000,000	cost of the London Docklands light railway.
76,000,000	saving to the UK government from ending the 'indiscriminate' subsidy of overseas students.
75,000,000	amount saved by restrictions on which medicines may be prescribed by general practitioners.

75,000,000	proceeds from the sale of surplus Ministry of Defence land.
74,700,000	road repair bill for the East Midlands.
74,168,000	value of a pile of £50 notes as high as St Paul's Cathedral.
74,012,000	UK imports from the United Arab Emirates.
73,640,000	UK exports to Iceland.
73,000,000	estimated annual savings in the National Health Service from using outside contractors.
71,624,000	UK imports from Brunei.
70,900,000	amount earned by Birmingham University from selling courses.
70,671,598	cost of buying a pint of beer for everyone in Mexico.
70,000,000	amount spent buying mineral water.
69,500,000	subscription (by solicitors) to the Law Society insurance fund.
69,400,000	Foreign Office expenditure on commercial work overseas (mainly promoting British business interests).
69,094,640	value of £10 notes placed end to end from London to Lisbon.
68,500,000	sale of Wembley Stadium.
67,459,000	UK exports to Chile.
67,100,000	road repair bill in Wales.
67,000,000	fees earned by accountants Grant Thornton.
66,949,000	UK exports to the Canary Islands.
66,670,000	value of a 100-m (328 ft) pile of £20 notes.
66,129,000	UK imports from Iraq.

66,500,000	UK imports from Fiji.
65,419,000	UK imports from Morocco.
65,000,000	amount private banks provided for private rented housing.
64,200,000	road repair bill in the north of England.
63,529,000	UK imports from the Canary Islands.
63,100,000	amount earned by Liverpool University from selling courses.
63,000,000	amount spend by London boroughs on bed and breakfast accomodation for the homeless.
62,869,000	UK exports to Tanzania.
62,491,823	what one second's flow over the Niagara Falls would be worth if it were whisky rather than water.
61,937,000	UK exports to Zimbabwe.
61,800,000	fees earned by accountants Binder Hamlyn.
60,400,000	fees earned by accountants KMG Thomson McLintock.
59,855,000	UK imports from St Lucia.
58,760,000	UK exports to Cuba.
58,517,000	UK imports from Kuwait.
58,149,000	UK exports to North Yemen.
58,084,000	UK exports to Colombia.
56,983,000	UK imports from Malawi.
56,000,000	cost of rebuilding the 14-year-old Royal Devon and Exeter Hospital.
56,000,000	amount the Post Office charge the BBC for collecting television licence fees.
55,867,000	UK exports to Lebanon.

55,756,800	cost of buying a Mars bar for everyone living in the USSR.
55,600,000	amount collected in development land tax.
55,535,000	UK imports from Guyana.
55,511,000	UK exports to Syria.
55,025,098	cost of buying a pint of beer for everyone in Germany.
55,000,000	value of the alleged Posgate fraud on Lloyd's.
55,000,000	UK government grants to help the poor with home insulation.
54,000,000	fees earned by accountants Spicer and Pegler.
53,400,000	amount collected in excise duty on cider and perry.
53,000,000	amount spent on cellular telephones.
52,900,000	amount earned by Bristol University from selling courses.
51,900,000	amount earned by Southampton University from selling courses.
51,860,000	UK imports from Sri Lanka.
51,474,335	cost of buying a pint of beer for everyone in Italy.
51,000,000	Bill Cosby's earnings for 1986 and 1987.
51,000,000	amount spent by Islington Council to create 4,167 jobs.
51,000,000	deficit of the Inner London Education Authority.
50,870,000	UK imports from Uganda.
50,512,498	cost of buying a pint of beer for everyone in the UK.
50,049,000	UK exports to Ethiopia.

50,000,000	UK government expenditure for tackling AIDS.
50,000,000	amount spent on home security.
50,000,000	Liverpool Council's budget deficit.
49,900,000	cost of the UK government's Restart programme.
49,766,000	UK imports from Jordan.
49,751,188	cost of buying a pint of beer for everyone in France.
49,620,000	UK exports to Puerto Rico.
49,197,000	UK imports from Malta.
48,800,000	amount earned by Belfast University from selling courses.
48,700,000	cost of the new Visa Interchange Centre for processing credit card transactions.
48,275,000	UK exports to Peru.
48,218,000	UK exports to Bangladesh.
48,194,000	UK imports from Swaziland.
48,000,000	UK government grant to Manchester University.
47,800,000	profit of Royal Insurance and General Accident group.
47,672,998	cost of buying a pint of beer for everyone in Thailand.
47,500,000	compensation awarded by a US court to the model Marla Hanson for a razor attack on her face.
46,673,000	UK exports to Ecuador.
46,200,000	UK exports to Gibraltar.
46,000,000	value of the fund set up to redeem pre-1917 Russian bonds.

45,700,000	Jaguar Cars' profit.
45,500,000	profits of B & Q stores.
45,500,000	the Church of England's income from stock exchange investments.
45,286,000	UK imports from Macao.
45,000,000	amount paid by direct debit.
44,975,000	UK exports to Panama.
44,800,000	UK government grant given to each of Oxford University, Glasgow University and Edinburgh University.
44,800,000	the Church of England's income from property investment.
44,099,998	cost of buying a pint of beer for everyone in Egypt.
43,900,000	UK goveroment grant to Cambridge University.
43,900,000	profits from Littlewoods mail order business.
43,800,000	income from court fines and fees in the first quarter of 1987/88.
43,378,000	UK exports to Jamaica.
43,147,000	UK imports from Angola.
43,100,000	UK government grant to Leeds University
42,700,000	Oxfam's income (highest of any charity).
42,400,798	cost of buying a pint of beer for everyone in England.
42,000,000	estimated cost of draught-proofing 300,000 homes on a Manpower Services Commission scheme.
42,000,000	deficit on the Vatican accounts at the end of 1986.
41,622,000	UK imports from Trinidad and Tobago.

41,613,312	cost of buying a Mars bar for everyone living in the USA.
41,500,000	loss made by Jebsens Drilling.
41,366,000	UK imports from Uruguay.
41,000,000	road repair bill for East Anglia.
40,642,000	value of 1,000 tons of 20p coins.
40,000,000	estimated annual saving to the Ministry of Defence by using private contractors.
40,000,000	ITV companies' contribution to Welsh Channel 4.
40,000,000	marketing cost of selling British Gas shares. The cost was criticised by the National Audit Office.
40,000,000	VAT income from the theatre.
40,000,000	UK government aid to Afghan rebels in Pakistan since 1979.
39,824,000	UK exports to Tunisia.
38,474,000	UK imports from Papua New Guinea.
38,338,000	UK exports to Barbados.
38,100,000	UK government grant to Birmingham University.
38,000,000	fees earned by accountants Pannell Kerr Forster.
38,000,000	amount paid by News International for *Today* newspaper.
38,000,000	cost of work overseas necessary to process claims for entry into the UK.
37,900,000	UK government grant to Liverpool University.
37,631,000	value of 1,000 tons of 50p coins.

37,300,000	amount Warwick University earned by selling courses.
37,000,000	cost of the Esso Fawley pipeline to the Midlands.
36,642,000	UK imports from Gabon.
36,000,000	amount Prince Thompson Akintole of Nigeria (unsuccessfully) tried to swindle from Midland Bank.
36,000,000	profits of Hilton International.
35,300,000	amount Xavier Gardinier, a vintner, is suing Chevron for in respect of the loss of three years' vintage through chemical contamination.
35,000,000	pensions paid by the Church of England.
34,936,518	cost of buying a pint of beer for everyone in Spain.
34,368,000	UK exports to Cameroon.
34,266,000	UK exports to Cuba.
34,217,000	UK exports to Zaire.
34,117,000	UK imports from Bangladesh.
34,048,000	price of 10,000 tons of mint imperials.
34,000,000	UK government expenditure on refugee relocation.
34,000,000	UK government spending on advertisements in the press in the year before the general election of 1987.
33,482,699	cost of buying a pint of beer for everyone in Poland.
33,436,000	annual cost of keeping prisoners in police cells.
33,330,000	value of a 100-m-high (328 ft) pile of £10 notes.

33,152,000	price of 10,000 tons of Nuttalls Mintoes.
33,000,000	Britoil's profits.
32,800,000	profit of the Save the Children charity.
33,006,000	cost of buying a Mars bar for everyone living in Indonesia.
32,459,000	UK imports from Bulgaria.
32,200,000	UK government grant to Newcastle University.
32,100,000	fees earned by accountants Moores and Rowland.
32,087,000	UK exports to Mauritius.
31,900,000	UK government grant to Sheffield University.
31,700,000	amount Leicester University earned from selling courses.
31,360,000	price of 10,000 tons of Liquorice Allsorts.
31,298,000	UK imports from Syria.
31,010,000	UK exports to Paraguay.
31,000,000	proceeds from the sale, in April 1987, of the Duchess of Windsor's jewellery.
30,896,000	UK exports to Angola.
30,464,000	price of 10,000 tons of Turkish delight.
30,318,000	UK imports from Costa Rica.
30,000,000	UK government grant to Bristol University.
30,000,000	value of food exported from the UK.
29,587,000	UK imports from Qatar.
29,400,000	fees earned by accountants Clark Whitehill in the year.
29,152,799	cost of buying a pint of beer for everyone in South Africa.

29,000,000	cost of the new civic centre for Gateshead Borough Council.
28,900,000	Salford University's income from selling courses.
28,800,000	income of the Royal National Lifeboat Institution.
28,635,000	UK imports from Argentina.
28,557,000	UK exports to Malawi.
28,500,000	what Next paid to buy Dillons (newsagents).
27,900,000	UK government grant to Nottingham University.
27,700,000	state lottery win (record) in Pennsylvania. The winner waited four months before she could pluck up the courage to claim her winnings.
27,700,000	Southwark Council's rent arrears.
27,600,000	fees earned by accountants Stoy Hayward in the year to 31 December 1986.
27,500,000	estimated loss made by the 126 editions of *London Daily News*.
27,260,000	UK imports from Zambia.
27,200,000	cost to UK of overseas consuls.
27,000,000	Sussex University's income from selling courses.
26,880,000	price of 10,000 tons of fudge.
26,612,000	UK imports from Dominica.
26,180,000	UK exports to Bermuda.
26,046,000	UK exports to Uganda.
26,000,000	estimated cost to the National Health Service of treating injured pedestrians.

26,000,000	amount spent by the British Overseas Trade Board.
25,984,000	price of 10,000 tons of liquorice comfits.
25,840,000	price of 10,000 tons of chocolate.
25,800,000	UK government grant to Southampton University.
25,700,000	estimated cost to the National Health Service of treating motorcycle injuries.
25,460,527	cost of buying a Polo mint for everyone in the world.
25,350,000	cost of maintaining Mrs Thatcher's offices since 1979.
25,000,000	underestimate in the building cost of the new British Library near St Pancras, London.
25,000,000	annual income of American comedian, Bill Cosby.
25,000,000	losses made by Greenwell Montagu, the market–makers owned by the Midland Bank before the Midland Bank withdrew in March.
25,000,000	amount spent on DIY plumbing items.
25,000,000	extra funds given by the UK government to the National Health Service, in February, to reduce waiting lists by 100,000.
24,900,000	Bradford University's income from selling courses.
24,750,000	price paid for the painting *Sunflowers* by Van Gogh, in April 1987, then a record for any painting.
24,465,000	UK exports to Uruguay.
24,348,000	cost of buying a Mars bar for everyone living in Japan.
23,928,000	UK exports to South Yemen.

23,892,000	UK imports from Guinea.
23,640,000	UK government investment in 'hot rock' technology in Cornwall.
23,500,000	UK government grant to Strathclyde University.
23,500,000	amount contractors had to pay back to the Ministry of Defence as 'excess profits'.
23,400,000	amount China agreed to pay in settlement of Chinese bonds issued before the Communist takeover.
23,000,000	annual pension contribution of Lucas Aerospace forgone in a pension holiday.
22,400,000	estimated annual income of actor Sylvester Stallone.
22,343,000	UK imports from Ethiopia.
23,215,499	cost of buying a pint of beer for everyone in California.
22,300,000	UK government grant to Aberdeen University.
22,056,000	UK exports to Liberia.
22,000,000	development expenditure of Cellnet to enable it to increase the carrying capacity of its existing channels.
22,000,000	amount saved by limiting doctors' choice of prescription for cough and cold remedies.
21,900,000	ticket sales for local authority lotteries in 1986.
21,800,000	amount spent on answering machines.
21,600,000	fees earned by accountants Neville Russell.
21,380,000	UK imports from the Faroe Islands.
21,253,000	amount staked on Zetters Pools.
21,230,000	UK exports to Martinique.

21,161,000	UK imports from St Vincent.
21,000,000	what BP paid for the onshore oilfields of Trafalgar House.
20,810,699	cost of buying a pint of beer for everyone in Yugoslavia.
20,683,251	amount paid for the Duchess of Windsor's jewellery on the first day of sale (about five times the estimated value).
20,600,000	fees earned by accountants Robson Rhodes.
20,000,000	liabilities of Sampart Sethia, who was declared bankrupt.
20,000,000	amount unpaid on the third instalment of TSB shares.
20,000,000	loss made by Austin Rover cars.
20,000,000	cost of the new Moss Bros headquarters.
20,000,000	profit-sharing bonus which British Telecom decided not to pay its staff after they went on strike.
20,000,000	amount lost by British Coal in unofficial disputes.
19,746,899	cost of buying a pint of beer for everyone in Morocco.
19,732,000	UK imports from Bahrain.
19,400,000	fees earned by accountants Moore Stephens.
19,100,000	UK government grant to Reading University.
19,000,000	price paid for the 0.64–acre (2,590 sq m) site of Kensington Barracks.
19,000,000	amount saved by restricting doctors' choice of painkillers in prescriptions.
18,800,000	UK government grant to Warwick University.

18,500,000	UK government grant to Loughborough University.
18,300,000	UK government's income from excise duty on matches and mechanical lighters.
18,300,000	value of a line of 5p coins placed edge to edge from London to San Francisco.
18,300,000	UK government grant to Leicester University.
18,300,000	Essex University's income from selling courses.
18,299,700	cost of buying a pint of beer for everyone in Kenya.
18,000,000	fees earned by accountants Hodgson Impey.
18,000,000	cost of treating UK patients with AIDS.
18,000,000	value of the Filofax company.
18,000,000	target set by the Church of England for its Church Urban Fund.
18,000,000	the Queen's income from overseas investments.
17,954,000	UK imports from Belize.
17,774,000	UK exports to Antigua.
17,730,000	cost of buying a pint of beer for everyone in Peru.
17,500,000	UK government grant to Durham University.
17,488,000	UK exports to Togo.
17,452,000	value of £10 notes laid end to end from London to Darlington.
17,403,000	UK exports to Sierra Leone.
17,300,000	net amount left in the will of Lady Macdonald–Buchanan, racehorse owner.

17,292,000	UK imports from Tunisia.
17,260,000	UK exports to Curaçao.
17,200,000	UK government grant to Cardiff University.
17,200,000	value put on the Filofax company when it was floated.
17,192,000	UK imports from Zaire.
16,950,000	estimated annual income of Bruce Springsteen.
16,707,000	UK exports to Gambia.
16,665,000	value of a 100-m-high (328 ft) pile of £5 notes.
16,650,000	estimated annual income of Charles M. Schultz, cartoonist and creator of the *Peanuts*-cartoon strip.
16,652,000	UK imports from Botswana.
16,627,000	UK exports to Gabon.
16,322,400	cost of buying a pint of beer for everyone in Afghanistan.
16,000,000	value of Capital Radio at flotation.
15,971,400	cost of buying a pint of beer for everyone in New York State.
15,704,800	cost of buying a Mars bar for everyone living in Mexico.
15,700,000	UK government grant to Exeter University.
15,554,000	UK imports from Surinam.
15,500,000	value wiped off the Hong Kong Stock Exchange on 26 October 1987 – about one third of the whole exchange's value.
15,400,000	Keele University's income from selling courses.
15,178,000	UK exports to the Dominican Republic.

15,150,000	estimated annual income of comedian Eddie Murphy.
15,100,000	UK government grant to Aston University.
15,020,000	EMAP's profit.
15,000,000	amount saved by restricting doctors' choice of what sedatives may be prescribed.
15,000,000	cost of developing the Connect debit card.
15,000,000	annual sale of postal orders.
15,000,000	Paul Getty's donation to the British Film Institute.
15,000,000	UK government grant to each of East Anglia University and Dundee University.
15,000,000	cost of bringing out the Jaguar XJ6 in the USA.
15,000,000	sale proceeds of the company Disctec, compact disc manufacturers.
15,000,000	Sainsbury's donation to plant research.
14,900,000	UK government grant to Bradford University.
14,805,264	cost of buying a Polo mint for everyone in Asia.
14,700,000	payments made in UK for medical negligence made by the Medical Defence Union.
14,500,000	redundancy bill for the last three years for the Welsh Water Authority. It now employs 132 more people than it did three years ago.
14,500,000	UK government grant for Sussex University.
14,400,000	UK government grant for Hull University.
14,286,000	UK imports from the Falkland Islands.
14,250,000	estimated annual income of pop singer Madonna.

14,010,000	price of 10,000 tons of ice cream.
13,950,000	cost of buying a pint of beer for everyone in Czechoslovakia.
13,900,000	UK government grant to Lancaster University.
13,881,000	UK imports from Senegal.
13,737,000	UK exports to Guyana.
13,600,000	UK government grant for Bath University.
13,300,000	estimated annual income of pop singer Whitney Houston.
13,219,426	what one second's flow over the Niagara Falls would be worth if it were wine rather than water.
13,200,000	UK government grant to Brunel University.
13,200,000	Bahamas' trade deficit.
13,175,000	UK exports to Mozambique.
13,174,000	UK exports to Andorra.
13,100,000	UK government grant to Salford University.
13,035,600	cost of buying a pint of beer for everyone in the Netherlands.
13,000,000	UK government grant to Surrey University.
13,000,000	estimated annual income of pop singer Michael Jackson.
13,000,000	amount Camden Council raised from selling its parking meters in a leaseback deal.
12,830,000	surplus (profit) made by Lloyd's Corporation.
12,826,000	UK imports from Sudan.
12,629,790	cost of buying a pint of beer for everyone in Australia.
12,650,000	price paid on 29 June 1987 for Le Pont de Trinquentaille by Van Gogh.

12,537,000	UK exports to Djibouti.
12,500,000	value of shares floated in the company Tie Rack.
12,441,000	UK exports to St Lucia.
12,328,000	UK exports to Senegal.
12,227,800	cost of buying a Mars bar for everyone living in Germany.
12,100,000	estimated annual income of American chat-show host Johnny Carson.
12,084,000	UK exports to Papua New Guinea.
12,007,000	UK exports to Costa Rica.
12,000,000	operating profit of Atomic Energy Authority (its first year as a commercial enterprise).
12,000,000	UK government payment to the BBC for monitoring overseas broadcasts.
12,000,000	amount spent on radio pagers.
11,913,000	UK imports from Afghanistan.
11,700,000	UK government grant to Warwick University.
11,661,000	UK imports from Barbados.
11,600,000	value of Babygro, the baby clothing company.
11,600,000	Bejam's profits.
11,599,000	UK imports from Sierra Leone.
11,444,250	value of £10 notes placed end to end from London to Sheffield.
11,444,000	UK exports to Afghanistan.
11,438,742	cost of buying a Mars bar for everyone living in Italy.
11,403,000	UK exports to the Cayman Islands.

11,339,000	UK imports from Ecuador.
11,300,000	UK government grant to St Andrews University.
11,225,000	cost of buying a Mars bar for everyone living in the UK.
11,200,000	insurance claims for theft of cash.
11,135,000	UK exports to the Falkland Islands.
11,100,000	Kwik-Fit's profits.
11,055,820	cost of buying a Mars bar for everyone living in France.
11,000,000	Gwent Council's road repair budget.
11,000,000	UK government grant to Bangor University.
11,000,000	monthly payout on premium bonds.
11,000,000	amount spent by the political parties in the general election campaign of 1987.
10,960,000	Brent Council's rent arrears.
10,900,000	UK government grant to Kent University.
10,800,000	UK government grant to Heriot–Watt University.
10,728,980	value of £10 notes placed end to end from London to Cardiff.
10,695,200	value of 100 tons of £1 coins.
10,679,000	UK exports to Guinea.
10,835,000	UK exports to Burma.
10,594,000	cost of buying a Mars bar for everyone living in Thailand.
10,367,000	UK exports to Niger.
10,266,000	UK imports from the Bahamas.
10,225,000	UK imports from Bolivia.

10,200,000	UK government grant to Aberystwyth University.
10,115,000	UK exports to Argentina.
10,102,500	cost of postage to send a first-class letter to everyone in the UK.
10,035,200	value of 1 ton of gold.
10,000,000	initial estimated value of a theft from Knightsbridge Safe Deposit Centre, London in July. (It was later revised to £30m.)
10,000,000	planned UK government expenditure on teaching entrepreneurial skills at universities and colleges.
10,000,000	annual cost of supplying diabetics with free syringes (introduced in 1 September 1987).
10,000,000	budget for regulation by the Securities Association.
9,845,000	UK imports from Lebanon.
9,800,000	cost of buying a Mars bar for everyone living in Egypt.
9,743,000	UK exports to Surinam.
9,639,000	UK exports to the Seychelles.
9,600,000	insurance claims for goods lost in transit.
9,516,947	what one second's flow over Niagara Falls would be worth if it were beer instead of water.
9,500,000	net estate of pop artist Andy Warhol.
9,422,400	cost of buying a Mars bar for everyone living in England.
9,337,893	value of 5p coins placed edge to edge from London to Tehran.
9,288,000	UK exports to Guatemala.

9,213,000	UK exports to Honduras.
9,206,100	cost of buying a pint of beer for everyone in Portugal.
9,180,000	cost of buying a pint of beer for everyone in Cuba.
9,165,000	UK exports to the Congo.
9,139,000	UK exports to Somalia.
9,000,000	street value of cocaine seized from a house in Harley Street, London in June 1987.
9,000,000	asking price for the 75-year lease on a 40-room house in St John's Lodge, Regents Park, London.
9,000,000	amount of drug-dealing profits recovered from banks when the law changed, compelling bank managers to reveal such information.
8,983,000	value of 1,000 tons of 10p coins.
8,873,005	cost of buying a pint of beer for everyone in Belgium.
8,797,764	value of £10 notes placed end to end from London to Nottingham.
8,780,000	UK exports to Dominica.
8,775,000	UK exports to Fiji.
8,750,000	annual salary of Steven Ross, head of Warner Communications.
8,700,000	UK government grant to Essex University.
8,642,350	value of a pile of £5 notes as high as Nelson's Column.
8,629,000	UK exports to Botswana.
8,628,000	UK exports to Grenada.
8,555,000	UK imports from Cuba.

8,549,640	value of a line of new pennies placed edge to edge from London to Sydney.
8,500,000	UK government grant to Keele University.
8,480,160	cost of postage to send a first-class letter to everyone in England.
8,288,000	UK exports to St Vincent.
8,282,000	UK imports from Mali.
8,232,000	UK exports to Belize.
8,200,000	UK government grant to Stirling University.
8,154,060	value of £10 notes placed end to end from London to Bristol.
8,098,000	UK imports from Guatemala.
8,000,000	total receipts for the play No Sex Please, We're British in the 16 years it ran, to its last performance on 5 September 1987.
8,000,000	amount won by student Miss Melanie Richards in the New York State Lottery.
8,000,000	value of tobacco companies' sponsorship of sport.
8,000,000	advertising budget for buying shares in British Airports Authority.
8,000,000	amount Camden Council raised by selling its library books in a leaseback deal.
7,760,000	amount spent by the Overseas Development Agency in supporting volunteers working on overseas development projects.
7,710,000	profits earned by Guinness Peat from insurance broking.
7,670,000	uncollected rents owed to Liverpool City Council.
7,522,325	cost of buying a pint of beer for everyone in Sweden.

7,487,000	UK imports from Rwanda.
7,763,671	cost of buying a Mars bar for everyone living in Spain.
7,634,000	UK imports from Cameroon.
7,599,000	UK imports from the Dominican Republic.
7,574,000	UK imports from Liberia.
7,500,000	increase in profits of Sears Holdings (who own Selfridges) resulting from a change in the way they value properties.
7,444,060	cost of buying a Mars bar for everyone living in Poland.
7,296,249	cost of postage to send a second-class letter to everyone in the UK.
7,166,700	cost of buying a pint of beer for everyone in Guatemala.
7,349,000	UK exports to Nicaragua.
7,165,000	arrears of mortgage payments owed to the Halifax Building Society (January.)
7,017,000	the National Gallery's planned expenditure for 1987/88.
7,011,000	UK imports from Grenada.
7,000,000	advertising budget to promote shares in the Channel Tunnel.
7,000,000	value of cuts which the UK government demanded be made by Brent Council.
6,972,000	UK exports to Aruba.
6,966,000	UK imports from Nepal.
6,959,600	value of a pile of £10 notes as high as Cleopatra's Needle.
6,917,000	UK exports to El Salvador.

6,885,103	value of 2p coins placed edge to edge from London to Mexico City.
6,872,000	UK exports to Madagascar.
6,826,000	UK imports from Namibia.
6,800,000	UK government grant to the Welsh Medical School.
6,799,500	cost of buying a pint of beer for everyone in Austria.
6,728,000	UK exports to Benin.
6,667,000	value of a 10-m-high (33 ft) pile of £20 notes.
6,522,000	UK exports to Macao.
6,500,000	initial funds of *News on Sunday*, launched on 26 April.
6,500,000	turnover of the Filofax company.
6,478,400	cost of buying a Mars bar for everyone living in South Africa.
6,448,268	cost of buying a pint of beer for everyone in New York City.
6,432,000	UK imports from Madagascar.
6,300,000	UK government expenditure on research into food crops for developing countries.
6,300,000	cost of the two drills to bore the Channel Tunnel.
6,158,313	amount left in the will of Alan Butler, the man who saved the aircraft company de Havilland from financial ruin in 1921.
6,124,559	cost of postage to send a second-class letter to everyone in England.
6,100,000	Jaguar Cars' expenditure on development.
6,096,000	value of a pile of £5 notes as high as the Monument.

6,092,000	UK imports from Burma.
6,087,600	cost of buying a pint of beer for everyone in Greater London.
6,079,000	income of the charity War on Want.
6,021,000	UK imports from Gibraltar.
6,000,000	street value of 95 lb (43 kg) of heroin seized in Essex in January.
6,000,000	debts of Containerworld when it went into liquidation (April.)
6,000,000	Sultan of Brunei's donation to President Reagan's fund for the Nicaraguan Contras.
6,000,000	amount spent by Anchor on promoting butter.
5,900,000	advertising budget for the 'Royal Event' unit trust.
5,836,320	cost of buying a pint of beer for everyone in Switzerland.
5,800,000	fees collected by overseas British consuls.
5,786,100	cost of buying a pint of beer for everyone in Bolivia.
5,780,000	uncollected rents owed to Manchester Council.
5,709,000	UK exports to the Faroe Islands.
5,700,000	cost of policing the printing and journalists' dispute at Wapping.
5,559,000	uncollected rents owed to Haringey Council.
5,553,000	amount spent by the charity War on Want.
5,500,000	amount spent by the Manpower Services Commission on a literacy training programme.
5,448,960	value of new pennies placed edge to edge from London to Singapore.

5,289,500	total cost of the Civil List (the amount the UK government provides for the royal family).
5,280,000	UK imports from Honduras.
5,159,000	cost of buying a Mars bar for everyone in California.
5,147,000	UK exports to Haiti.
5,008,000	UK imports from Togo.
5,000,000	estimated cost of damage done to Ministry of Defence property in the October 1987 hurricane.
5,000,000	estimated daily cost of alcoholism.
5,000,000	amount spent by Barclays Bank promoting its Connect card.
5,000,000	amount US television evangelist Oral Roberts said he needed by the end of March to stop God 'taking him back'. He raised the money and God did not take him back.
5,000,000	amount raised for charity under the payroll giving scheme.
5,000,000	cost of vandalism to farms.
5,000,000	amount Tower Hamlets Council spent housing Bangladeshi families in hotels.
4,950,000	UK imports from Panama.
4,950,000	cost of buying a pint of beer for everyone in Hong Kong.
4,929,408	value of a line of pennies placed edge to edge from London to Tokyo.
4,910,000	UK imports from Benin.
4,900,000	annual cost of the Securities Investment Board.
4,848,000	UK imports from South Yemen.

4,816,700	value of £1 coins placed edge to edge from London to Exeter.
4,789,000	UK imports from Greenland.
4,750,000	UK imports from Mongolia.
4,700,000	value wiped off securities owned by Warburg Securities on 19 October 1987.
4,672,000	UK exports to Nepal.
4,624,600	cost of buying a Mars bar for everyone in Yugoslavia.
4,623,300	cost of buying a pint of beer for everyone in Scotland.
4,612,315	cost of buying a pint of beer for everyone in Denmark.
4,533,365	value of £1 coins placed edge to edge from London to Sheffield.
4,516,200	cost of buying a pint of beer for everyone in Chad.
4,500,000	amount raised for charity in the seventh London Marathon.
4,500,000	estimated saving to the BBC from moving its headquarters' staff to White City.
4,500,000	outstanding debts of Cardiff University.
4,417,200	cost of buying a pint of beer for everyone in Finland.
4,389,264	value of new pennies placed edge to edge from London to Mexico City.
4,388,200	cost of buying a Mars bar for everyone in Morocco.
4,326,100	the Civil List payment to the Queen.
4,121,000	UK exports to Mali.
4,074,000	UK imports from the Solomon Islands.

4,066,600	cost of buying a Mars bar for everyone in Kenya.
4,000,000	amount the British Museum needs to strengthen its floors.
4,000,000	value of sponsorship withdrawn by *Today* newspaper from the Football League.
4,000,000	money raised for the restoration of Ely Cathedral.
4,000,000	estimated cost to the Church of England if the 50% rebate, currently enjoyed on vicarage rates, was to be withdrawn under the proposed Community Charge (poll tax).
4,000,000	amount spent by Kent Council in clearing snow.
4,000,000	losses made by Mercury, the telecommunications competitor to British Telecom.
3,940,000	cost of buying a Mars bar for everyone in Peru.
3,926,000	UK exports to Montserrat.
3,922,000	UK exports to Swaziland.
3,900,000	redundancy payment made by Midland Bank to Frank Cahouet.
3,839,940	cost of buying a pint of beer for everyone in Israel.
3,840,000	amount paid in October, at Christie's, for a 2-in (5 cm) long flawless diamond.
3,790,910	value of £10 notes placed end to end from London to Brighton.
3,663,000	UK exports to Bolivia.
3,627,200	cost of buying a Mars bar for everyone in Afghanistan.
3,549,200	cost of buying a Mars bar for everyone in New York State.

3,520,000	UK exports to New Caledonia.
3,500,000	estimated compensation paid to the 100 known victims of Legionnaires' Disease.
3,500,000	annual subscriptions from trade unions to the Labour Party.
3,500,000	cost of press advertising by the Conservative Party during the general election of 1987.
3,479,800	value of a pile of £5 notes as high as Cleopatra's Needle.
3,477,000	UK exports to Guadeloupe.
3,466,628	cost of buying a pint of beer for everyone in Canada.
3,404,800	price of 1,000 tons of mint imperials.
3,333,000	value of a 10-m-high (33 ft) pile of £10 notes.
3,331,000	UK exports to North Korea.
3,315,200	price of 1,000 tons of Nuttalls Mintoes.
3,312,900	cost of buying a pint of beer for everyone in Paraguay.
3,267,000	amount paid in October 1987 for a Gutenberg Bible dating from 1455.
3,200,302	amount raised by the Cavalry and Guards Club, Piccadilly, London to buy its premises and fend off a redevelopment. A photostat of the cheque hangs among the club's paintings.
3,154,000	UK exports to US Oceania.
3,136,000	price of 1,000 tons of Liquorice Allsorts.
3,115,000	amount paid by the Tate Gallery for *The Weeping Woman* by Picasso.
3,104,000	UK exports to Burkina Faso.
3,100,000	cost of buying a Mars bar for everyone in Czechoslovakia.

3,074,000	UK imports from Burundi.
3,046,400	price of 1,000 tons of Turkish delight.
3,004,411	what one second's flow over the Niagara Falls would be worth if it were lemonade rather than water.
3,000,000	donation from the Wellcome Trust for medical research.
3,000,000	annual amount spent by British Rail in heating railway points.
3,000,000	estimated loss from *The Evening News* in its brief rebirth, from February to October 1987.
3,000,000	estimated cost of the annual general meeting of British Gas.
3,000,000	estimated cost of the unfinished and insolvent National Jazz Centre in London.
3,000,000	parental contributions to student grants.
2,986,800	price of 1,000 tons of Dolly Mixtures.
2,976,376	cost of buying a pint of beer for everyone in New Zealand.
2,946,687	value of £1 coins placed edge to edge from London to Bournemouth.
2,920,000	cost of foreign visits made by Mrs Thatcher since 1979.
2,915,000	UK exports to Namibia.
2,900,000	Marks and Spencer's donations to charity.
2,896,800	cost of buying a Mars bar for everyone in the Netherlands.
2,887,000	UK exports to Albania.
2,870,000	cost of training a Royal Navy Sea Harrier pilot.
2,850,850	value of 1,000 tons of new pennies.

2,806,620	cost of buying a Mars bar for everyone in Australia.
2,806,000	UK imports from Chad.
2,790,000	UK government contribution to the World Health Organisation programmes connected with health and population research.
2,787,049	cost of buying a pint of beer for everyone in Los Angeles.
2,762,000	UK exports to Ceeta and Melilla.
2,737,152	value of new pennies placed edge to edge from London to New York.
2,688,000	price of 1,000 tons of fudge.
2,640,000	UK government compensation paid to farmers after the Chernobyl disaster.
2,600,000	estimated cost of repairing vandalised telephone boxes.
2,598,400	price of 1,000 tons of liquorice comfits.
2,584,000	price of 1,000 tons of chocolate.
2,530,800	cost of buying a pint of beer for everyone in Wales.
2,500,000	estimated amount Andrew Warburg swindled from his clients in the firm Norton Warburg.
2,500,000	cost of electrifying the railway line from Kings Cross to Cambridge.
2,500,000	amount paid by *Sunday Sport* for the building used by the Communist newspaper *Morning Star*.
2,500,000	advertised annual rent for 4,500 sq ft (418 sq m) of office space in the City of London (May 1987).
2,496,000	UK exports to Mauritania.
2,444,000	UK imports from the Congo.

2,422,000	UK imports from Cayman Islands.
2,407,020	total prize money offered at Wimbledon lawn tennis tournament.
2,327,580	cost of buying a pint of beer for everyone in Singapore.
2,324,000	UK exports to Burundi.
2,300,000	cost of Lambeth Council's minimum wage policy.
2,284,039	net amount left in the will of Charles David Darley, a retired brewery chairman.
2,273,000	UK imports from Gambia.
2,250,000	amount saved by Merton Council by using private contractors.
2,247,057	what one second's flow over Niagara Falls would be worth if it were 4-star petrol instead of water.
2,200,000	cost of security for the Pope's visit to the USA.
2,184,000	UK imports from Mauritania.
2,181,682	value of £1 coins placed edge to edge from London to Southampton.
2,168,496	value of new pennies placed edge to edge from London to Tehran.
2,147,928	price paid for the painting *Pink Lady* by William de Kooning; a record for a work by a contemporary artist.
2,128,000	UK exports to Lesotho.
2,106,000	UK imports from North Yemen.
2,100,000	loss made on estate agency business by the Prudential Corporation.
2,100,000	premium paid to use the Body Shop trademark in the USA.

2,096,681	value of £1 coins placed edge to edge from London to Dover.
2,092,500	cost of buying a pint of beer for everyone in Jamaica.
2,069,000	UK imports from Antigua.
2,045,800	cost of buying a Mars bar for everyone in Portugal.
2,040,000	cost of buying a Mars bar for everyone in Cuba.
2,000,000	expenditure on food at Henley Regatta.
2,000,000	price paid for a five-bedroom terraced house with a mews cottage and roof garden, over-looking Regents Park, in July.
2,000,000	overdraft of Earl of Haddington which, in May, forced him to sell his ancestral home.
2,000,000	amount paid for Calderstone Comprehensive School, Liverpool (John Lennon's old school) for development into a Tesco's store.
2,000,000	amount of cocaine given to a drug pusher by HM Customs and Excise in an unsuccessful attempt to track a major network.
2,000,000	amount the British Rail pension fund received for selling 98 old master prints.
2,000,000	estimated cost of a fire at St Peter's Church, Eaton Square, London.
1,971,779	cost of buying a Mars bar for everyone in Belgium.
1,962,450	cost of buying a pint of beer for everyone in Panama.
1,900,000	UK government grant to the London Business School.
1,870,013	value of £1 coins placed edge to edge from London to Northampton.

71

1,870,000	value of Investors Newsletter in the bid made by Publishing Holdings. Investors Newsletter's accounts showed assets of £53,000.
1,812,500	amount paid for the Duchess of Windsor's 31-carat diamond ring, the highest price for any of her jewellery.
1,800,000	estimated maximum amount embezzled from Pitman's, the secretarial course company, over 20 years by Charles McGuire, the company's bookkeeper.
1,711,000	UK imports from Guadeloupe.
1,710,000	cost of buying a pint of beer for everyone in Mongolia.
1,700,000	amount spent by the Home Office in advertising home security, using magpies.
1,681,000	UK exports to Rwanda.
1,671,628	cost of buying a Mars bar for everyone in Sweden.
1,670,087	net amount left in the will of Lady McAlpine, wife of the civil engineering boss.
1,667,000	value of a 10-m-high (33 ft) pile of £5 notes.
1,618,000	UK exports to the Cape Verde Islands.
1,618,000	UK exports to the Solomon Islands.
1,600,000	UK government donation to the International Planned Parenthood Federation for its research into AIDS.
1,600,000	value of Courage Brewery's sponsorship of rugby.
1,592,600	cost of buying a Mars bar for everyone in Guatemala.
1,587,678	value of £1 coins placed edge to edge from London to Oxford.

1,585,830	value of 1p invested at 5% in 1600.
1,524,000	value of a 1-yd-high (91 cm) pile of £50 notes.
1,511,000	cost of buying a Mars bar for everyone in Austria.
1,501,677	value of £1 coins placed edge to edge from London to Brighton.
1,500,000	asking price for the 60-tonne catamaran used in the James Bond film *The Living Daylights*.
1,500,000	cost of the UK government 'Look After Your Heart' campaign, launched on 21 April.
1,500,000	advertising budget for the new gold Britannia coin.
1,500,000	amount British Telecom said it would save if all its customers paid by direct debit.
1,500,000	debts of Lambeth Council's direct labour organisation.
1,500,000	the Labour Party's press advertising costs during the last general election campaign.
1,460,000	UK exports to Laos.
1,460,000	payments from the Depositors Protection Board against the three banks that became insolvent.
1,455,000	UK imports from Paraguay.
1,452,000	UK imports from the Central African Republic.
1,432,948	cost of buying a Mars bar for everyone in New York City.
1,402,200	cost of buying a pint of beer for everyone in Northern Ireland.
1,401,000	price of 1,000 tons of ice cream.
1,400,000	cost of a one-way ring road in Glasgow, partly opened in July.

1,400,000	contract awarded to News UK to print a colour version of the *News of the World* instead of *Sunday Today*.
1,400,000	price paid on 25 June 1987 for the painting *Bouquet de Fleurs* by Claude Monet; a record for one of his works.
1,400,000	ITV's budget to improve its image.
1,400,000	value of stolen property, mostly fine arts, found at the home of Brian Reddington.
1,400,000	nominal value of the Kestrel pension scheme. The receiver only found £400,000.
1,400,000	lump sum paid by CBS to its former chairman Thomas Wyman.
1,400,000	face value of forged Eurobonds in Exxon, bought by Goldman Sachs, the American securities house.
1,389,690	cost of buying a pint of beer for everyone in Hampshire.
1,382,000	amount spent by the UK government, in April, advertising its job creation programmes.
1,374,000	UK imports from North Korea.
1,369,000	UK imports from Burkina Faso.
1,354,230	cost of buying a pint of beer for everyone living in Essex.
1,352,800	cost of buying a Mars bar for everyone in Greater London.
1,335,000	UK imports from Mozambique.
1,326,677	value of 5p coins placed edge to edge from London to Glasgow.
1,323,000	UK imports from El Salvador.
1,321,000	UK exports to the Maldives.

1,319,000	UK exports to Guinea–Bissau.
1,312,000	amount paid for the Duchess of Windsor's emerald engagement ring.
1,307,000	UK imports from Nicaragua.
1,300,000	cost of rebuilding St Stephen's Church, Wallbrook.
1,296,960	cost of buying a Mars bar for everyone in Switzerland.
1,288,000	UK exports to Vietnam.
1,285,800	cost of buying a Mars bar for everyone in Bolivia.
1,262,000	UK imports from Bermuda.
1,250,000	UK exports to Chad.
1,242,270	cost of buying a pint of beer for everyone living in Lancashire.
1,239,000	UK exports to Nauru.
1,233,144	value of new pennies placed edge to edge from London to Moscow.
1,210,000	amount paid in June for a Knole desk (a record price for a single item of furniture).
1,200,000	UK imports from Vietnam.
1,191,680	worth of Robert Maxwell's weight in gold.
1,136,000	UK exports to Anguilla.
1,128,000	annual salaries of Jim and Tammy Bakker, disgraced television evangelists from PTL ministries, USA.
1,100,000	price paid for a full-length portrait of Lt-Col Jonathan Bullock, painted by Gainsborough.
1,100,000	cost of buying a Mars bar for everyone in Hong Kong.
1,100,000	deficit on overseas passport and consul fees.

1,100,000	cost of building a road to the village of Rhenigidale, on the Isle of Harris – Europe's remotest village.
1,100,000	UK government grant to Manchester Business School.
1,099,000	UK exports to the Vatican City.
1,095,087	cost of buying a Polo mint for everyone in the USA.
1,069,520	value of 100 tons of £1 coins.
1,059,177	debt run up by a 23-year-old trainee accountant, earning £6,400 a year, when his investments crashed in October.
1,052,000	UK exports to French Guyana.
1,037,000	UK exports to Vanuatu.
1,032,088	record pools win by a London housewife in April.
1,032,000	record damages, awarded in July to Samir Aboul-Hosn, for a surgeon's error which turned him into a 'zombie'.
1,031,000	UK exports to Mongolia.
1,027,400	cost of buying a Mars bar for everyone in Scotland.
1,025,000	UK exports to the Turks and Caicos Islands.
1,024,959	cost of buying a Mars bar for everyone in Denmark.
1,015,092	cost of buying a pint of beer for everyone living in Botswana.
1,003,600	cost of buying a Mars bar for everyone in Chad.
1,001,959	cost of removing illegal immigrants from Britain.
1,000,000	amount Stanley Royd psychiatric hospital

wasted on a 'cook-chill' catering system found to be unhygienic. The hospital bought the system as an economy measure.

992,681 value of 20p coins placed edge to edge from London to Northampton.

981,600 cost of buying a Mars bar for everyone in Finland.

971,000 profit made by Spurs football team.

950,000 annual salary of Jim Bakker, disgraced television evangelist from the PTL network in the USA.

938,000 UK imports from the Seychelles.

936,000 UK exports to Tonga.

924,660 cost of postage to send a first-class letter to everyone in Scotland.

920,000 price of a diamond-studded swimsuit on sale in Japan.

912,000 UK exports to the Pitcairn Islands.

910,260 cost of buying a pint of beer for everyone living in Surrey.

900,000 Ealing Council's funding of London Strategic Policy Unit.

899,100 cost of buying a pint of beer for everyone living in Devon.

899,000 UK imports from Haiti.

898,332 value of 100 tons of 10p coins.

880,000 amount paid for the 45-sq-yard (37.6 sq m) painting *Midwinterblot* by Carl Larsson.

875,000 cost of policing the Notting Hill Carnival.

850,000 amount the Ministry of Agriculture is spending on researching mushrooms.

840,000	amount which John Fleming was accused of handling from the £26m Brinks Mat gold robbery. It took magistrates 25 seconds to acquit him on 25 June.
853,320	cost of buying a Mars bar for everyone in Israel.
848,000	UK imports from Niger.
829,650	net amount left in the will of Sir Gordon Richards, racehorse trainer and jockey.
817,000	UK exports to the British Indian Ocean Territories.
800,000	value of stock misappropriated from Tip Top Drugstores.
797,153	value of new pennies placed edge to edge from London to Brighton.
790,000	one year's aid from Britain to combat locusts and army worms in Ethiopia.
787,000	UK exports to the Central African Republic.
784,888	amount paid for the Duchess of Windsor's Cartier panther bracelet.
771,600	expenses incurred by the Foreign Compensation Commission since its formation in 1986. It has yet to pay out any compensation to anyone.
770,362	cost of buying a Mars bar for everyone in Canada.
765,072	value of new pennies placed edge to edge from London to Lisbon.
760,000	amount which Fife Regional Council had to sue from the £1.1m it lent to striking coalminers
750,769	net amount left in Ted Moult's will.

750,000	amount paid to UK 2000, a UK government community programme.
750,000	UK government grant to the European Year of the Environment.
746,000	Glaxo's profit.
740,000	UK imports from Somalia.
725,000	value of the painting *Madonna and Child* by Giovanni Bellini, which the state accepted in lieu of taxes.
736,200	cost of buying a Mars bar for everyone in Paraguay.
706,464	value of new pennies placed edge to edge from London to Rome.
705,846	auction room price for a manuscript by Gaston Phébus (a record for a fifteenth-century manuscript).
700,000	salary of Ian Posgate, nicknamed 'Goldfinger', until he was dismissed for his part in a fraud at Lloyd's.
675,000	price paid in the UK for a 2-cent stamp (record for a stamp).
674,000	UK exports to the polar regions.
670,000	amount the UK government spent in advertising its cold weather payments.
667,810	cost of postage to send a second-class letuer to everyone in Scotland.
667,000	value of a 1-m-high ($3\frac{1}{3}$ ft) pile of £20 notes.
661,417	cost of buying a Mars bar for everyone in New Zealand.
650,000	payment Midland Bank made to the National Union of Mineworkers in settlement of a legal action for breach of trust in managing pension funds in 1984.

643,000	weekly cost of keeping prisoners in police cells.
641,000	unpaid debts for private medicine, written off by National Health Service hospitals.
640,737	cost of buying a Polo mint for everyone in Japan.
633,000	UK exports to Equatorial Guinea.
630,000	UK government funding to the opposition parties.
655,020	cost of buying a pint of beer for everyone living in Norfolk.
625,000	advance royalty payment to Michael Holroyd for a biography of George Bernard Shaw. (The previous record for an advance royalty was £90,000.)
622,000	UK imports from Western Samoa.
615,000	profits of Babygro, the baby clothing company.
619,344	cost of buying a Mars bar for everyone in Los Angeles.
609,600	value of 1-yd-high (0.9 m) pile of £20 notes.
608,000	price paid for 1,000 flower engravings used to illustrate *Hortus Eystettensis* (record price for a botanical book).
605,880	value of new pennies placed edge to edge from London to Madrid.
605,790	cost of buying a pint of beer for everyone living in Cyprus.
600,000	offer from pop singer Michael Jackson to London Hospital for the remains of the Elephant Man. The offer was declined.
600,000	amount the Labour Party intended to save by laying off 30 of its headquarters staff.

582,300	cost of buying a pint of beer for everyone living in Swaziland.
576,000	UK imports from Aruba.
575,000	liabilities of the football club Tranmere Rovers when it nearly went bust in February.
562,400	cost of buying a Mars bar for everyone in Wales.
560,000	damages paid to Jonathan Rudge, a 21-year-old student, for a motor accident in 1981.
550,000	compensation awarded to a 14-year-old girl for serious brain damage caused by hospital negligence.
530,000	redundancy payments made by J. E. Hanger & Co. Ltd, ending the long-running dispute at the limb-making factory.
524,000	UK imports from Australian Oceania.
517,240	cost of buying a Mars bar for everyone in Singapore.
515,000	compensation paid to William Tomkin who suffered brain damage after falling from a scaffold tower in 1981.
508,000	value of 1-ft-high (30.48 cm) pile of £50 notes.
507,856	net amount left in the will of Joseph Samuels, pioneer of the radio taxi.
506,160	cost of postage to send a first-class letter to everyone in Wales.
506,000	UK exports to Mayotte.
502,380	cost of buying a pint of beer for everyone living in Cleveland.
500,000	damages awarded to Jeffrey Archer against *The Star* for its allegations that he slept with a prostitute.

L

500,000	cost of cleaning graffiti from London Underground stations.
500,000	amount pledged by London businessmen to launch 'crime stopper'.
500,000	surcharge and costs imposed on the former Labour councillors of Liverpool.
500,000	annual salary of Terry Wogan (according to one newspaper).
500,000	donation from the Abbey National to the Open University to establish a chair of finance.
500,000	bail granted to Ronson for his part in the Guinness scandal.
488,000	UK exports to Australian Oceania.
483,912	value of new pennies placed edge to edge from London to Copenhagen.
470,880	cost of buying a pint of beer for everyone living in Bedfordshire.
468,072	value of new pennies placed edge to edge from London to Berlin.
465,000	cost of buying a Mars bar for everyone in Jamaica.
459,000	UK imports from the Pitcairn Islands.
454,500	cost of buying a pint of beer for everyone living in Alaska.
452,672	amount paid for the Duchess of Windsor's flamingo brooch.
452,000	UK exports to Greenland.
450,000	value of the painting *Vase of Flowers* by Renoir, stolen in April.
450,000	amount of fines written off every year in Birmingham.

440,355	amount the Labour Party received from the UK government.
436,100	cost of buying a Mars bar for everyone in Panama.
433,000	UK exports to Western Samoa.
430,000	profit of Tip Top Drugstores.
426,000	UK imports from Cape Verde Islands.
423,500	Arts Council grant to Bristol Old Vic (£70,000 less than the previous year).
418,968	value of new pennies placed edge to edge from London to Inverness.
413,284	cost of buying a Polo mint for everyone living in Mexico.
410,040	cost of buying a pint of beer for everyone living in Somerset.
406,420	value of 10 tons of 20p coins.
401,580	cost of buying a pint of beer for everyone living in Cornwall.
400,000	contribution Townsend Thorensen was ordered to make to the costs of the public inquiry into the Zeebrugge ferry disaster.
400,000	debts incurred by Robert Swan's expedition to the South Pole.
400,000	damages paid by the Metropolitan Police.
400,000	value of gold found in the toilet of a British Airways aeroplane in February.
400,000	amount spent on legal fees by Ian Posgate in fighting his fraud case.
400,000	the National Union of Mineworkers' donation to the Labour Party's 1987 election fund.
400,000	payments made to the Technical Change Centre, a research quango which the UK government abolished.

390,708	amount left in the will of Sir Hugh Carlton Greene, former director general of the BBC.
389,664	value of new pennies placed edge to edge from London to Aberdeen.
385,000	amount raised by the sale of the painting *Under the Birches* by Albert Ederfelt.
384,000	value of fashion clothes stolen from Krizia in Milan in March. They were found in April.
380,000	cost of buying a Mars bar for everyone in Mongolia.
376,310	value of 10 tons of 50p coins.
375,000	the Civil List payment to the Queen Mother.
365,560	cost of postage to send a second-class letter to everyone in Wales.
360,000	cost of buying a pint of beer for everyone living in Bristol.
360,000	sum stolen by five armed robbers wearing comic masks.
360,000	UK government's annual subsidy to two empty tower blocks in Canning Town, which Newham Council have declared as unfit for human habitation.
358,000	UK imports from Montserrat.
352,936	cost of printing early day motions on the House of Commons order papers.
351,270	cost of buying a pint of beer for everyone living in Shropshire.
350,000	amount paid for the Duchess of Windsor's fleur-de-lis diamond brooch.
350,000	amount paid by Elizabeth Taylor to buy the Duchess of Windsor's Prince of Wales' feathers clip.

350,000	value of Conservative Party advertisements declined by the *Daily Mirror*.
340,480	price of 100 tons of mint imperials.
340,000	amount saved by Woking Council from contracting out its vehicle fleet.
339,500	amount paid for the Duchess of Windsor's 1940 bib necklace.
333,300	value of a 1-m-high ($3\frac{1}{3}$ ft) pile of £10 notes.
331,520	price of 100 tons of Nuttalls Mintoes.
330,940	award to Christopher Peerless, a 23–year–old trainee naval mechanic, for brain damage suffered in a road accident.
330,332	payments made by the Metropolitan Police in out-of-court settlements.
329,310	cost of buying a pint of beer for everyone living in Luxembourg.
327,530	value of 10p coins placed edge to edge from London to Canterbury.
327,000	UK exports to Niue and Tokelau.
321,814	cost of buying a Smartie for everyone in India.
320,000	proceeds of sale of cricket memorabilia at Lords on 13 April.
316,800	value of new pennies placed edge to edge from London to Frankfurt.
315,000	cost of UK government legal action in the three years to June 1987, to stop the publication of the books *Spycatcher*, by Peter Wright, and *One Girl's War*, by Joan Miller.
313,600	price of 100 tons of liquorice comfits.
313,500	amount paid on 24 July for the draft of a secret treaty made between Charles II and Louis XIV of France.

311,600	cost of buying a Mars bar for everyone in Northern Ireland.
308,820	cost of buying a Mars bar for everyone in Hampshire.
308,088	value of new pennies placed edge to edge from London to Glasgow.
307,000	UK exports to the Comoros.
306,659	amount left in the will of Air Marshal Sir Robert Victor Goddard, technical specialist in the Dunkirk evacuation.
304,800	value of a 1-yd-high (0.9 m) pile of £10 notes.
304,640	price of 100 tons of Turkish delight.
300,940	cost of buying a Mars bar for everyone in Essex.
300,000	credit facilities which were withdrawn by Citibank from Pineapple Dance Studios.
300,000	loss made by the *Morning Star*.
300,000	value of Roy Hattersley's home (according to *The News of the World*).
299,294	value of 10p coins placed edge to edge from London to Brighton.
295,680	price of 100 tons of Dolly Mixtures.
294,294	value of new pennies placed edge to edge from London to Edinburgh.
289,695	net amount left in the will of Bill Rickaby, jockey.
287,370	cost of buying a pint of beer for everyone living in Croydon.
287,000	UK imports from US Oceania.
283,256	value of 2p coins placed edge to edge from London to Blackpool.

279,000	UK exports to the Cook Islands.
277,000	UK imports from Lesotho.
276,000	UK imports from the Maldives.
276,060	cost of buying a Mars bar for everyone in Lancashire.
273,240	cost of buying a pint of beer for everyone living in Belfast.
273,230	auction price of *Le Roy Modus*; a record for French incubala.
273,000	appeal costs paid by Price Waterhouse to accountancy disciplinary bodies, for its inefficient and incompetent auditing of Bryanston Finance, a secondary bank.
271,293	net amount left in the will of Harold Rosenthal, former editor of *Opera* magazine.
268,800	price of 100 tons of fudge.
265,000	amount paid for the Duchess of Windsor's 1935 diamond bracelet bearing nine crosses.
264,000	sale proceeds of a mosaic, measuring $18\frac{1}{2}$ by 14 in (46.25 x 35 cm) dated 1070, and found in a Welsh village church.
260,000	amount paid for the Duchess of Windsor's jewellery bearing the engraved message 'hold tight'.
259,800	price of 100 tons of liquorice comfits.
258,400	price of 100 tons of chocolate.
254,000	value of a 6-in (15 cm) pile of £50 notes.
251,010	cost of buying a pint of beer for everyone living in Cardiff.
250,000	amount spent by Steven Morgan hiring the London Palladium for an ill-attended Christian crusade.

250,000	estimated cost of unsuccessful legal action by the National Union of Mineworkers on whether pension contributions should be considered in assessing compensation.
250,000	amount which Haringey Council and Brent Council each invested from their pension funds in *News on Sunday*.
250,000	cost to the Metropolitan Police of their computer system HOLMES (Home Office Large Major Enquiry System) for co-ordinating information on serious crimes.
250,000	annual payments into the Prince's Trust.
250,000	net liquid assets you must have to get a gold Visa card from Adam & Co.
250,000	amount spent by Haringey Council in investigating freemasonry.
250,000	amount spent by Camden Council in promoting homosexuality.
250,000	maximum premium bond prize.
246,912	amount paid for the Duchess of Windsor's collection of diamond cufflinks and buttons.
245,760	award to Maria Woolerton, a gymnast, for a road accident which left her dumb and almost blind.
242,000	cost of a railway snow plough.
240,000	UK government's purchase of sheep to monitor the consequences of the Chernobyl nuclear disaster.
236,000	UK imports from Niue and Tokelau.
234,450	cost of buying a pint of beer for everyone living in Wandsworth.
233,640	value of new pennies placed edge to edge from London to Carlisle.

231,000	auction price for the painting *Mountains of Rondane* by Harald Scholberg.
230,000	amount raised in a public appeal for the sur-charged Liverpool councillors by the end of March.
228,060	cost of buying a pint of beer for everyone living in Plymouth.
228,000	cost of official entertainment by Mrs Thatcher since 1979.
226,000	value of the Nobel prize for chemistry.
225,000	cost of extending the Kent and East Sussex railway line by 2 miles (3.2 km).
225,576	cost of buying a Mars bar for everyone in Botswana.
220,000	price paid for a grandfather clock in April, (record).
219,328	cost of buying a pint of beer for everyone living in Iceland.
217,008	value of new pennies placed edge to edge from London to Newcastle-upon-Tyne.
217,000	UK exports to Kampuchea.
216,891	net amount left in the will of Stephen Barry, a former valet of the Prince of Wales.
214,000	UK imports from Guinea-Bissau.
212,000	Tower Hamlets Council's arts budget.
210,000	value of advertising in the press spent by the Alliance Parties during the last general election.
209,300	the Civil List payment to the Duke of Edinburgh.
205,760	amount paid for a miniature photograph of Queen Victoria, inscribed 'from great grand-mama VR1 24 May 1899'.

203,200	value of a 1-ft-high (30.48 cm) pile of £20 notes.
202,280	cost of buying a Mars bar for everyone in Surrey.
201,908	cost of buying a Smartie for everyone living in England.
201,775	price paid for the painting *Egyptian Café* by David Hockney; a record for one of his works.
200,000	minimum amount Guy's Hospital expects to earn each year from a privately run pay-bed scheme.
200,000	amount raised for the Zeebrugge ferry disaster by the record 'Let It Be' in its first nine days.
200,000	estimated cost to the taxpayer of one fatal road accident
199,800	cost of buying a Mars bar for everyone in Devon.
195,624	value of a line of new pennies placed edge to edge from London to Truro.
195,000	amount which Cyril Smith, the Liberal MP, obtained from selling his spring-making company.
193,770	cost of buying a pint of beer for everyone living in Derby.
193,500	cost of buying a pint of beer for everyone living in Southwark.
193,160	Avon Council's grant to the Bristol Old Vic.
192,674	cost of buying a pint of beer for everyone living in Aberdeen.
188,000	amount spent by Reigate Council in using 17 tons of sand to fill caves and mines to prevent subsidence.

182,160	value of a line of new pennies placed edge to edge from London to Amsterdam.
182,070	cost of buying a pint of beer for everyone living in Southampton.
180,755	value of a line of 5p coins placed edge to edge from London to Brighton.
180,576	value of a line of new pennies placed edge to edge from London to Blackpool.
180,000	the amount Ian Wood, a solicitor, admitted stealing from clients. He also killed his lover and her two children. He was arrested in a French cathedral.
179,000	UK exports to Kiribati.
176,500	proceeds from selling Holywood Hall Hospital, Durham to a property developer.
175,000	amount of the divorce settlement payable to Conservative MP John Browne.
175,000	salary of the chairman of the British Gas Corporation.
174,946	net amount left in the will of Joan Lascelles, lady-in-waiting to Princess Alice.
170,000	saving achieved by not using cones on motorways as proposed.
170,000	EEC donation to the Zeebrugge ferry disaster fund.
170,000	Anne Diamond's annual salary.
169,454	net amount left in the will of George Hart, actor.
169,110	cost of buying a pint of beer for everyone living in Portsmouth.
168,660	cost of buying a pint of beer for everyone living in Swansea.

91

167,904	value of a line of new pennies placed edge to edge from London to Aberystwyth.
166,700	value of a 1-m-high ($3\frac{1}{3}$ ft) pile of £5 notes.
164,608	amount paid for the Duke of Windsor's ruby-studded cigarette case bearing a map of his European train journeys.
163,989	gross takings of *Crocodile Dundee* in its first week; a record for a West End première.
163,000	shortfall discovered in the accounts of Aberdeen Steak Houses, which led to police investigation.
156,816	value of a line of new pennies placed edge to edge from London to Liverpool.
156,575	net amount in the will of Wing Cdr Vera Thomas, curator of the Prime Minister's home, Chequers.
155,000	prize for the men's singles winner at Wimbledon lawn tennis tournament.
152,400	value of a 1-yd-high (0.9 m) pile of £5 notes.
151,600	value of a 6-in-high (15 cm) pile of £20 notes.
151,272	value of a line of new pennies placed edge to edge from London to Leeds.
150,000	UK imports from Laos.
150,000	start-up costs for *Sunday Sport*.
150,000	maximum lump sum payment under the new pension laws.
149,688	value of a line of new pennies placed edge to edge from London to Swansea.
149,449	net amount left in the will of Sir John Burgess, former chairman of Reuters.
148,500	price paid on 24 June for a first edition of *Alice Through the Looking Glass* by Lewis Carroll.

148,500	price paid for the painting *Fisherman Pulling A Boat* by Kroyer.
148,000	UK imports from Nauru.
147,993	cost of buying a pint of beer for everyone living in Milton Keynes.
145,728	value of a line of new pennies placed edge to edge from London to Manchester.
145,560	cost of buying a Mars bar for everyone in Norfolk.
143,019	cost of buying a pint of beer for everyone living in Basildon.
142,659	value of Britannia gold coins sold by the Britannia Building Society in their first two weeks (14–28 October).
140,100	price of 100 tons of ice cream.
140,000	grant to Scotland's first centre for sexually abused children, in Yorkhill.
139,000	prize for ladies' singles winner at Wimbledon lawn tennis tournament.
138,000	the Civil List payment to the Duke of Kent.
137,000	value of a writ issued by the Multi Commercial bank of Geneva against Conservative MP Edward du Cann.
136,350	cost of buying a pint of beer for everyone living in Macclesfield.
135,432	value of a line of new pennies placed edge to edge from London to Hull.
134,620	cost of buying a Mars bar for everyone in Cyprus.
134,620	value of a line of new pennies placed edge to edge from London to Exeter.
131,500	the Civil List payment to Princess Alexandra.

131,220	cost of buying a pint of beer for everyone living in Blackpool.
130,400	the Civil List payment to the Princess Royal.
130,000	price paid on 22 June for Edward VIII's McLaughlin Buick.
129,870	cost of buying a pint of beer for everyone living in Bournemouth.
129,497	net amount left in the will of David Penhaligon, Liberal MP.
129,400	cost of buying a Mars bar for everyone in Swaziland.
129,000	UK imports from Albania.
127,000	amount paid by Lee International to buy Moores and Griffin, a special effects company.
127,000	the Civil List payment to Princess Margaret.
126,720	value of a line of new pennies placed edge to edge from London to Sheffield.
125,000	amount a husband or wife will inherit if their partner has not made a will and is survived by parents or brothers or sisters, but not children.
125,001	retirement relief for capital gains tax.
124,000	annual budget of Camden Council's homosexuality unit.
122,000	amount Richard Atterton, managing director of Containerworld, is alleged to have obtained by deception prior to the company's liquidation.
120,330	cost of buying a pint of beer for everyone living in Maidstone.
120,000	payment by a Hackney Council sponsored 'charity' towards buying a hotel in the West Indies.

118,800	value of a line of new pennies placed edge to edge from London to Cardiff.
115,920	cost of buying a pint of beer for everyone living in St Albans.
114,120	cost of buying a pint of beer for everyone living in Lancaster.
112,893	value of 3 tons of 50p coins.
112,770	cost of buying a pint of beer for everyone living in Guildford.
110,070	cost of buying a pint of beer for everyone living in Norwich.
110,000	average price of a three-bedroom semi-detached house in Rickmansworth (June).
108,180	cost of buying a pint of beer for everyone living in Ipswich.
106,952	value of 1 ton of £1 coins.
104,940	cost of buying a pint of beer for everyone living in Chester.
104,640	cost of buying a Mars bar for everyone in Bedfordshire.
104,580	cost of buying a pint of beer for everyone living in Oxford.
104,328	cost of buying a Smartie for everyone in Canada.
103,000	amount Dr Ranbit Singh Vaid defrauded from the National Health Service.
102,899	cost of buying a pint of beer for everyone living in Canterbury.
101,600	value of 1-ft-high (30 cm) pile of £10 notes.
101,000	cost of buying a Mars bar for everyone in Alaska.

101,000	arrears of rent owed by the House of Hartnell, the Queen's dressmakers, when they became insolvent.
100,000	maximum award the building societies ombudsman may award against a building society.
100,000	legal costs of the unsuccessful action by ratepayers against Waltham Forest's 62% rate increase.
100,000	amount wagered, two days before the 1987 general election, on a Conservative victory. William Hill then refused to accept any more bets on a Conservative victory.
100,000	amount Brent Council budgeted to spend in proving that it is not barmy.
100,000	salary of the chairman of the British Steel Corporation.
100,000	bail for Ian Posgate, held on Lloyd's fraud charge.
100,000	fines imposed on its members by the London International Financial Futures Exchange in August, for breach of tax rules.
100,000	average price of a three-bedroom semi-detached house in St Alban's (in June).
99,768	net amount of the will of Sir Edward Youde, former governor of Hong Kong.
97,416	value of a line of new pennies placed edge to edge from London to Nottingham.
95,000	UK imports from French Polynesia.
95,000	cost of the investigation into the John Stalker affair.
94,140	cost of buying a pint of beer for everyone living in Stratford-on-Avon.

92,058	average cost of a semi-detached house in Greater London (October).
91,800	cost of buying a pint of beer for everyone living in Exeter.
91,170	cost of buying a pint of beer for everyone living in Carlisle.
91,120	cost of buying a Mars bar for everyone in Somerset.
90,228	value of a line of new pennies placed edge to edge from London to Bristol.
90,000	price paid by a wedding-car hire company for the converted white landrover used as a 'pope-mobile' in England in 1982.
90,000	amount which can be inherited before inheritance tax becomes payable.
89,833	value of 10 tons of 10p coins.
89,567	net amount left in the will of Clifford Hoston, managing director of Rolls-Royce.
89,240	cost of buying a Mars bar for everyone in Cornwall.
88,830	cost of buying a pint of beer for everyone living in Cambridge.
88,704	value of a line of new pennies placed edge to edge from London to Norwich.
88,641	UK government funding of the Liberal Party.
88,000	UK imports from Tuvalu.
87,141	cost of buying a Smartie for everyone in Kenya.
86,435	salary of the Lord Chancellor, including his fees as Speaker of the House of Lords.
86,000	UK imports from Tonga.

86,000	UK imports from the Turks and Caicos Islands.
85,091	cost of buying a pint of beer for everyone living in Winchester.
82,929	bad debts written off by Camberwell Health Authority.
82,827	average price of a semi-detached house in Hertfordshire (October).
82,500	UK government grant to the homeless in Nicaragua.
82,368	value of a line of new pennies placed edge to edge from London to Bournemouth.
82,086	average price of a semi-detached house in Surrey (October 1987).
81,990	cost of buying a pint of beer for everyone living in Gloucester.
81,000	salary of the Lord Chief Justice.
80,000	cost of buying a Mars bar for everyone in Bristol.
80,000	cost of moving a Victorian lodge 7 yd (6.4 m) to widen the Popsham Road in Exeter.
80,000	amount Rochdale Council saved by contracting out its refuse collection services.
80,000	average amount an architect spends buying himself a house.
79,400	salary of the Lord Chancellor.
78,600	salary of the chairman of British Rail.
78,060	cost of buying a Mars bar for everyone in Shropshire.
78,000	UK exports to Tuvalu.
76,000	UK exports to Bhutan.

76,000	profit made in nine months from the purchase and sale of a council house in Purley, Surrey.
76,000	UK imports from the Vatican City.
75,655	average price of a semi-detached house in Berkshire (October).
75,500	amount spent on equipment to monitor the Chernobyl fall-out.
75,000	transfer fee for footballer Mark Dennis, paid by Queen's Park Rangers to Southampton.
75,000	average price of a semi-detached house in Hemel Hempstead (June).
75,000	legacy from a husband or wife to each other if they have made no will and leave children as well. (The person also inherits personal chattels and half the residue.)
74,750	salary of the Master of the Rolls.
73,180	cost of buying a Mars bar for everyone in Luxembourg.
72,191	cost of buying a pint of beer for everyone living in Jersey.
71,750	salary of a High Court judge, Queens Bench Division.
70,000	sponsorship from Lewisham Council to Milwall Football Club for its anti-racist and anti-sexist policies.
69,758	average price of a semi-detached house in West Sussex (October).
67,506	cost of buying a Smartie for everyone in Australia.
66,680	profit which three businessmen tried to make by fraudulently representing that 3,334 cases of Oxo cubes were for export.

65,862	cost of postage to send a letter to everyone in Luxembourg.
65,843	amount paid for the Duchess of Windsor's lorgnette (record).
65,000	fine imposed on Antonio Gruber, former banker at Morgan Guaranty Trust, for bank fraud.
65,000	salary of the chairman of the United Kingdom Atomic Energy Authority.
65,000	salary of the chairman of the Royal Mint.
65,000	salary of a High Court judge, Chancery and Family Divisions.
64,739	salary of the Ombudsman.
63,860	cost of buying a Mars bar for everyone in Croydon.
63,626	average value of a home in Greater London (September).
63,353	value of 1p invested at 5% in 1666.
63,317	average price of a semi-detached house in Oxford (October).
63,158	average price of a semi-detached house in Essex (October).
63,123	debts of the insolvent boxer Maurice Hope.
62,995	average price of a semi-detached house in Buckinghamshire (October).
62,562	UK government funding of the Social Democratic Party.
62,500	amount of wine and brandy drunk by four men employed at Fortnum and Mason, from paper cups during lunchtimes.
62,401	nct amount left in the will of Air Vice Marshall Stewart Menaul, aviation expert.

62,244	average price of a semi-detached house in East Sussex (October).
62,100	salary of a Grade 1 civil servant (permanent secretary).
62,100	salary of the commissioner of the Metropolitan Police.
62,000	UK imports from Vanuatu.
62,000	average price of a three-bedroom semi-detached house in High Wycombe (June).
61,598	average price of a semi-detached house in Kent (October).
60,984	value of a line of new pennies placed edge to edge from London to Southampton.
60,720	cost of buying a Mars bar for everyone in Belfast.
60,000	UK imports from Anguilla.
60,000	out-of-court settlement agreed in the USA by a pastor who called two members of his church adulterers in a sermon.
59,500	salary of the director-general of the British Council.
59,228	cost of postage to send a second-class letter to everyone in Somerset.
58,923	tax debts which bankrupted Maurice Hope, middleweight boxer.
58,608	value of a line of new pennies placed edge to edge from London to Dover.
58,529	cost of buying a pint of beer for everyone living in the Seychelles.
58,500	mortgage granted by Guardian Building Society to the Hell's Angels to buy a residence in Windsor for use as a clubhouse.

58,234	cost of buying a Smartie for everyone living in Ghana.
58,000	price paid in June for a house comprising one room 15 ft by 9 ft (4.5 x 2.7 m) with a tiny kitchen and toilet (but no bathroom) in Holland Park, London.
58,000	UK imports from Kampuchea.
57,854	cost of buying a pint of beer for everyone living on the Isle of Man.
57,215	amount awarded in April to a policeman who suffered a crippling knee injury in a street riot in 1981.
56,800	annual salary of a Grade 1A civil servant (second permanent secretary).
56,232	value of line of new pennies placed edge to edge from London to Portsmouth.
56,000	amount spent by Haringey Council on a cat hostel.
55,780	cost of buying a Mars bar for everyone in Cardiff.
55,000	UK imports from French Guyana.
55,000	compensation to a woman who was wrongly sterilised as a teenager.
55,000	average price of a three-bedroom semi-detached house in Bedford (June).
55,000	sale proceeds for the VC awarded to PO Thomas Gould, the first man to shoot down a Zeppelin in the First World War.
54,696	cost of buying a pint of beer for everyone living in Inverness.
54,000	average price for a house paid by a first-time buyer in London (July).
54,000	annual salary of the government actuary.

54,000	UK imports from British Indian Ocean Territories.
53,837	cost of buying a Polo mint for everyone in Portugal.
53,000	UK imports from Djibouti.
52,588	net amount left in the will of Pat Phoenix, the actress who played Elsie Tanner in *Coronation Street*.
52,272	value of a line of new pennies placed edge to edge from London to Northampton.
52,100	cost of buying a Mars bar for everyone in Wandsworth.
52,000	cost of postage to send a second-class letter to everyone in Bristol.
51,400	the Civil List payment to Princess Alice, Duchess of Gloucester.
50,800	value of a 1-ft-high (30 cm) pile of £5 notes.
50,680	cost of buying a Mars bar for everyone in Plymouth.
50,000	damages awarded against the Ward family when their Labrador dog jumped at a man, causing him to fall into the path of a passing car.
50,000	the Civil List payment to Prince Andrew.
48,750	salary of the Speaker of the House of Commons.
48,739	cost of buying a Mars bar for everyone in Iceland.
48,523	salary of an Italian politician.
47,900	average price paid for a UK house (July).
47,546	compensation paid to a woman who had a 30-in (75 cm) length of stomach-pump tube left in her stomach after an operation.

47,000	Ritz–Hemingway prize for the best novel, won by Peter Taylor for his book *A Summons to Memphis*.
46,000	amount paid for Elvis Presley's 1968 gold Cadillac.
46,000	UK imports from the Cook Islands.
45,936	value of a line of new pennies placed edge to edge from London to Canterbury.
45,612	cost of postage to send a letter to everyone in Plymouth.
45,000	UK imports from New Caledonia.
45,000	value of 100,000 Australian dollars, which a family in Melbourne found, attached by rubber bands to branches of the trees in their garden.
45,000	salary of a lieutenant–general.
44,775	salary the Prime Minister is entitled to draw.
44,000	UK imports from Ceeta and Melilla.
43,560	value of a line of new pennies placed edge to edge from London to Oxford.
43,500	top salary for a Grade 2 civil servant (deputy secretary).
43,500	salary of a circuit judge.
43,060	cost of buying a Mars bar for everyone in Derby.
43,000	maximum salary of a British Airways airline captain.
43,000	cost of buying a Mars bar for everyone in Southwark.
43,000	UK imports from the polar regions.
42,857	cost of buying a Smartie for everyone in Nigeria.

42,816	cost of buying a Mars bar for everyone in Aberdeen.
42,350	value of a 1-in-thick (2.5 cm) pile of £50 notes.
42,000	net amount left in Lord Stockton's will.
41,976	value of a line of new pennies placed edge to edge from London to Brighton.
41,910	cost of buying a Polo mint for everyone who lives in Guatemala.
41,800	salary of the chairman of the Civil Aviation Authority.
41,509	cost of postage of sending a second-class letter to everyone in Croydon.
41,500	starting salary of a Grade 2 civil servant (deputy secretary).
41,200	amount of taxable income at which the 60% rate starts.
40,642	value of 1 ton of 20p coins.
40,460	cost of buying a Mars bar for everyone in Southampton.
40,000	amount raised by an impromptu collection among aeroplane passengers, for treatment for a four-year-old girl with a serious heart problem.
40,000	salary of the chief executive of Lambeth Council.
40,000	UK imports from Andorra.
40,000	amount which the Freemasons give to Church of England cathedrals each year.
40,000	price of an average house in the UK (September).
39,897	salary of a French politician.
39,000	a telephone bill which the Metropolitan Police refused to pay in protest at poor service.

38,000	amount paid by a Munich advertising agency for the Cessna light aircraft which Mathias Rust landed in Red Square, Moscow in May.
38,000	maximum amount payable for death on board a ferry under the Athens Convention.
37,631	value of 1 ton of 50p coins.
37,580	cost of buying a Mars bar for everyone in Portsmouth.
37,480	cost of buying a Mars bar for everyone in Swansea.
37,400	amount paid for a drawing by Constable of the Lake District.
37,216	compensation paid for an employee of British Nuclear Fuels Ltd, who died in 1973.
37,000	salary of a major-general.
36,500	price paid for a converted broom cupboard, measuring 5 ft 6 in by 11 ft (1.6 x 3.3 m), opposite Harrods.
36,460	salary of the Lord Advocate.
36,390	salary of the Leader of the House of Lords.
35,350	top salary for a Grade 3 civil servant (under secretary).
35,345	salary of the Attorney-General.
35,000	price paid in September for an eighteenth-century marquetry commode.
35,000	fictitious overtime payment claims made by staff at Lambeth Council's computer centre in Brixton.
35,000	average price paid by a fireman to buy a house.
35,000	largest reported donations to the Conservative Party – by Sun Alliance and Royal Insurance.

34,043	salary of a West German politician.
34,089	salary of a brigadier.
34,000	estimated cost of rescuing Richard Branson and his co-pilot when the Virgin Atlantic balloon was ditched in the sea.
33,820	salary of the chairman of the BBC.
33,300	amount of taxable income at which the 55% tax rate starts.
33,145	salary of a cabinet minister.
33,123	amount of English estate left in the will of Cary Grant.
32,874	cost of buying a Mars bar for everyone in Milton Keynes.
32,500	fines imposed by Lloyd's on Sir Peter Green, its chairman from 1980 to 1983, for discreditable conduct.
32,350	starting salary for a Grade 3 civil servant (under secretary).
31,782	cost of buying a Mars bar for everyone in Basildon.
31,500	cost of buying a pint of beer for everyone living in Rutland.
31,450	salary of a colonel after eight years.
31,070	net amount left in the will of the twelfth Earl of Huntley.
31,000	legal expenses of a court action brought by parents in Hawkins County, Tennessee, to stop the theory of evolution being taught in schools.
31,000	UK government grant paid to find out why whispering is distracting.
30,700	salary of a colonel after six years.

30,640	salary of a senior non-Cabinet minister.
30,475	top salary for a Grade 4 civil servant.
30,340	average pay of a surgeon.
30,300	cost of buying a Mars bar for everyone in Macclesfield.
30,297	salary of a Belgian politician.
30,250	price paid for the Lordship of the Manor of Old Buckenham, Norfolk. The holder gets £110 a year from the Electricity Board to allow electricity cables to be laid across the village green.
30,120	award made by the Onassis Foundation to Amnesty International for 'its outstanding humanitarian efforts'.
30,005	salary of the Archbishop of Canterbury.
30,000	price charged by a Swansea firm for a holiday of one day in space in 1992. The fee includes four days' space training. They were fully booked.
30,000	state funding of Harlow Unemployed Centre, which was withdrawn after they had repeatedly flouted the rules by using the centre for political purposes.
30,000	value of jewels stolen from the home of Ruud Lubbers, the Dutch prime minister.
30,000	amount paid by building societies to sponsor a crime prevention promotion.
30,000	amount paid for a car parking space in Spencer Walk, Hampstead.
30,000	maximum amount of a mortgage whose interest qualifies for income tax relief.
30,000	arrears of dividends owned by Jordan to prostitutes. In pre-war West Africa, many prosti-

tutes were paid with bearer warrants whose dividends have never been claimed.

30,000	average amount which a hairdresser pays for a house.
29,950	salary of a colonel after four years.
29,680	salary of the director of the National Portrait Gallery.
29,648	salary of a Dutch politician.
29,587	cost of postage to send a first-class letter to everyone in Milton Keynes.
29,199	salary of a colonel after two years.
29,160	cost of buying a Mars bar for everyone living in Blackpool.
29,000	amount of money which a man stole from a gambling club and then burned as a protest against gambling.
28,975	starting salary for a Grade 4 civil servant.
28,860	cost of buying a Mars bar for everyone living in Bournemouth.
28,625	salary of the Solicitor-General.
28,508	value of 10 tons of new pennies.
28,499	salary of a colonel on appointment.
28,086	average price of a semi-detached house in Derbyshire.
27,271	salary of a lieutenant-colonel after eight years.
27,255	salary of the chief whip.
27,100	price of a BMW 735i car from June.
27,065	top salary of a Grade 5 civil servant (assistant secretary).
26,949	average price of a house in Humberside (September).

26,740	cost of buying a Mars bar for everyone living in Maidstone.
26,623	salary of a lieutenant-colonel after six years.
26,411	cost of buying a Polo mint for everyone living in Chad.
26,244	cost of postage to send a first-class letter to everyone in Blackpool.
26,190	salary of the Archbishop of York.
25,975	salary of a lieutenant-colonel after four years.
25,760	cost of buying a Mars bar for everyone living in St Albans.
25,400	value of a 6-in-high (15 cm) pile of £5 notes.
25,400	amount of taxable income at which the 50% tax rate starts.
25,360	cost of buying a Mars bar for everyone living in Lancaster.
25,327	salary of a lieutenant-colonel after two years.
25,200	cost of buying a pint of beer for everyone living in Monaco.
25,060	cost of buying a Mars bar for everyone living in Guildford.
25,000	gross income needed to qualify for a gold card from Lloyds Bank, the Midland Bank or the Royal Bank of Scotland.
25,000	fine imposed on Geoffrey Collier for insider dealing.
25,000	fine imposed on Cargill Investor Services for breach of regulations on futures trading.
24,932	average price of a semi-detached house in Clwyd (October).
24,820	cost of buying a Mars bar for everyone living on the Isle of Wight.

24,679	starting salary of a lieutenant-colonel.
24,660	cost of buying a pint of beer for everyone living in Liechtenstein.
24,640	salary of a senior parliamentary secretary.
24,460	cost of buying a Mars bar for everyone living in Norwich.
24,427	cost of postage to send a second-class letter to everyone in Portsmouth.
24,382	salary of the chairman of the Forestry Commission.
24,355	salary of the Bishop of London.
24,314	salary of a Danish politician.
24,302	top salary of a Grade 6 civil servant (senior principal).
24,100	income level needed to be a 'top earner' as defined by the National and Provincial Building Society.
24,085	salary of the Solicitor-General for Scotland.
24,040	cost of buying a Mars bar for everyone living in Ipswich.
23,730	starting salary of a Grade 5 civil servant (assistant secretary.
23,320	cost of buying a Mars bar for everyone living in Chester.
23,240	cost of buying a Mars bar for everyone living in Oxford.
23,000	average profits of a one-man accountancy practice.
23,000	salary of the chairman of the North of Scotland Hydroelectricity Board.
23,000	typical bank manager's salary.

22,882	average price of a semi-detached house in County Armagh (October).
22,875	salary of a non-Cabinet minister.
22,864	cost of buying a Mars bar for everyone living in Canterbury.
22,548	MP's salary.
22,539	salary of a Luxembourg politician.
22,455	cost of buying a Polo mint for everyone in Israel.
22,000	minimum pay of a university professor.
21,700	salary of an oil executive at Shell.
21,636	cost of postage to send a first-class letter to everyone in Ipswich.
21,570	salary of a lord-in-waiting.
21,415	salary of the Bishop of Durham.
21,352	salary of a major after eight years.
21,300	annual turnover at which a business must register for VAT.
21,000	average salary of a financial controller.
21,000	grant given to lecturer Dr Margaret Stray to study tourism in Greece.
21,000	compensation paid by Lanarkshire Health Board for a failed vasectomy operation.
20,988	cost of postage to send a first-class letter to everyone in Chester.
20,920	cost of buying a Mars bar for everyone living in Stratford-on-Avon.
20,910	salary of a major after seven years.
20,467	salary of a major after six years.
20,400	cost of buying a Mars bar for everyone living in Exeter.

20,400	amount of taxable income at which the 45% rate starts.
20,397	government funding of the Ulster Unionist Party.
20,301	amount of taxable income which a married couple needs to earn before it is worthwhile considering being taxed separately.
20,260	cost of buying a Mars bar for everyone living in Carlisle.
20,140	MP's secretarial allowance.
20,125	cost of buying a pint of beer for everyone living in San Marino.
20,024	salary of a major after five years.
20,000	price paid by the state of Bolivia at Sotheby's to regain the diaries of Che Guevara, which they say were stolen.
20,000	cost of copying the list of British Telecom shareholders.
20,000	threshold of 'rich', per Labour Party.
20,000	price paid for the Lordship of the Manor of Liston, Essex. The holder is entitled to carry the wafers at a coronation.
20,000	price paid for a costume worn in 1916 by Olga Khokhlova, Picasso's wife.
20,000	the Civil List payment to Prince Edward.
20,000	amount spend by Bristol Council to see if it is worthwhile setting up a bank to cater for ethnic minorities.
19,800	salary of a Spanish politician.
19,740	cost of buying a Mars bar for everyone living in Cambridge.
19,581	salary of a major after four years.

113

19,500	average price paid by a first-time buyer for a house in the north (July).
19,500	amount borrowed by Keith Best for his illegal multiple applications for shares in British Telecom.
19,465	top salary of a Grade 7 civil servant (principal).
19,440	cost of buying a pint of beer for everyone living in the Cayman Islands.
19,138	salary of a major after three years.
18,909	cost of buying a Mars bar for everyone living in Winchester.
18,828	cost of postage for sending a first-class letter to everyone in Stratford-on-Avon.
18,809	salary of the chairman of the Countryside Commission.
18,695	salary of a major after two years.
18,508	average salary of a chief accountant.
18,252	salary of a major after one year.
18,234	cost of postage to send a first-class letter to everyone in Carlisle.
18,220	cost of buying a Mars bar for everyone living in Gloucester.
18,020	starting salary for a Grade 6 civil servant (senior principal).
18,000	average salary of a newly qualified accountant in London.
17,900	amount of taxable earnings at which the 40% income tax rate starts.
17,898	salary offered by Haringey Council for a heating engineer to work on the troubled Broadwater Estate in Tottenham.

17,810	salary of a major on appointment.
17,766	cost of postage to send a first-class letter to everyone in Cambridge.
17,730	salary of the Bishop of Winchester.
17,381	cost of postage to send a second-class letter to everyone in Maidstone.
17,343	damages awarded to Katrina Powling, a crash victim, against the driver of the other car, who was killed in the accident.
17,339	cost of buying a pint of beer for everyone living in the Orkney Islands.
17,309	salary of an Irish politician.
16,940	value of a 1-in-thick (2.5 cm) pile of £20 notes.
16,885	salary of a parliamentary secretary.
16,650	value of a 1-cm-thick (0.39 in) pile of £50 notes.
16,414	cost of buying a Smartie for everyone in Malta.
16,398	cost of postage to send a first-class letter to everyone in Gloucester.
16,272	salary of an army captain after six years.
16,050	average salary of a departmental chief accountant.
16,042	cost of buying a Mars bar for everyone living in Jersey.
16,000	average salary of a chief financial accountant.
16,000	cost of buying a Mars bar for everyone living in Eastbourne.
16,000	extra expenditure incurred on prison cells at Newbury police station, Berkshire, because they were originally built to open inwards, instead of outwards as required by law.

16,000	salary of a sex discrimination officer at Camden Council.
15,980	cost of buying a Mars bar for everyone living in Dartford.
15,925	salary of a diocesan bishop in the Church of England.
15,899	cost of postage for sending a second-class letter to everyone in Norwich.
15,895	salary of an army captain after five years.
15,750	average salary of a chief management accountant.
15,518	salary of an army captain after four years.
15,354	average annual wage of a buyer at the Wellcome Foundation.
15,141	salary of an army captain after three years.
15,000	fine imposed on Peter Robinson MP for 'invading' the village of Clontibret in the Republic of Ireland.
15,000	gross income needed to qualify for a Bank of Scotland gold card.
14,861	cost of postage for sending a second-class letter to everyone in Canterbury.
14,764	salary of an army captain after two years.
14,700	price paid in May for an angora goat.
14,400	cost of postage to send a first-class letter to everyone in Eastbourne.
14,387	salary of an army captain after one year.
14,377	cost of buying a Polo mint for everyone in Monaco.
14,318	starting salary for a Grade 7 civil servant (principal)

14,306	annual cost of educating one state school pupil to five 0-level passes in Newham.
14,173	cost of buying a Smartie for everyone in New Zealand.
14,100	salary of an architect employed by Birmingham City Council.
14,010	salary of an army captain on appointment.
14,000	UK imports from Martinique.
13,935	average salary of a chief cost accountant.
13,815	salary of the whips in the House of Commons.
13,598	cost of postage to send a second-class letter to everyone in Stratford-on-Avon.
13,480	advertised salary of a nuclear-free-zone co-ordinator for Brent Council.
13,223	average salary of a management accountant.
13,169	cost of postage to send a second-class letter to everyone in Carlisle.
13,150	average teacher's pay.
13,032	average salary of a financial accountant.
13,006	cost of buying a Mars bar for everyone living in the Seychelles.
13,000	refurbishment cost of the town hall at Blaenau, Gwent. (Nobody knows who ordered the refurbishment.)
12,965	salary of a dean or provost in the Church of England.
12,856	cost of buying a Mars bar for everyone living in the Isle of Man.
12,771	annual cost of educating one state school pupil to five 0-level passes in Inner London. The national average is £5,086.

12,396	amount which John Martin McAleese is accused of obtaining by deception. He was head of BBC finance in Northern Ireland.
12,276	salary of a lieutenant after four years.
12,154	cost of buying a Mars bar for everyone living in Inverness.
12,059	value of 1p invested at 5% in 1700.
12,000	damage done to Rotterdam trees by a stray dog biting them.
12,000	amount paid for the Duke of Windsor's gold pipe cleaner.
12,000	asking price for the Austrian title Baron de Rothenthal.
12,000	cost of policing Myra Hindley's return to the Yorkshire moors.
12,000	amount Haringey and Hackney Councils spent on 'Lesbian Strength and Gay Pride Festival' in June.
11,983	salary of a lieutenant after three years.
11,705	(median) average salary of a cost accountant.
11,696	annual cost of educating one state school pupil to five 0-level passes in Barking.
11,690	salary of a lieutenant after two years.
11,556	salary of a Greek politician.
11,400	purchasing power of the average American.
11,397	salary of a lieutenant after one year.
11,119	annual wage of a chef at Shell Chemicals.
11,104	salary of a lieutenant on appointment.
11,084	cost of buying a Smartie for everyone in Singapore.
11,000	price paid on 17 June for a set of Wisden's

almanacs, the cricketer's bible, covering the years 1864–1985.

10,975 average annual wage of a buyer at the Timex Corporation.

10,742 average salary of an investment analyst at the Scottish Mutual Assurance Society.

10,500 price paid for a broken saltpot made of Staffordshire slipware. It was bought for £2 at a car boot sale.

10,465 salary of a canon residentiary in the Church of England.

10,417 annual cost of educating one state school pupil to five O-level passes in Haringey.

10,400 average wage of a fireman.

10,400 purchasing power of the average Canadian.

10,332 salary of a Portuguese politician.

10,161 cost of buying a Smartie for everyone in the Bahamas.

10,048 cost of buying a Smartie for everyone living in Strathclyde.

10,030 purchasing power of the average Norwegian.

10,000 initial offer from P & O as compensation for each death on the *Herald of Free Enterprise*.

10,000 amount spent by Brent Council on installing a lift for the disabled at a school which has no disabled pupils, but has serious fabric decay.

10,000 bill sent to the Ministry of Defence by St Peter's Church, Fakenham Magna, for damage done by RAF Tornado fighters.

10,000 cost of a special snail-breeding shed.

9,966 cost of buying a Smartie for everyone living in Jamaica.

9,837	annual wages of a buyer at Pilkington Glass.
9,747	annual cost of educating one state school pupil to five 0-level passes in Waltham Forest.
9,700	purchasing power of the average resident of Luxembourg.
9,300	income level at which parents must contribute £40 to a student grant.
9,147	annual wage of a carpenter at Heinz.
9,000	minimum 'going rate' for a lordship of the manor, according to the Manorial Research Society.
9,000	UK imports from Mayotte.
9,000	going rate for a forged British passport.
8,983	value of 1 ton of 10p coins.
8,960	annual charge to an overseas student to study dentistry.
8,945	starting salary for a carpenter at Cable & Wireless plc.
8,800	purchasing power of the average Swede.
8,750	starting salary for an articled clerk (Coopers and Lybrand).
8,600	purchasing power of the average West German.
8,520	salary of a sub-lieutenant.
8,470	value of a 1-in-thick (2.5 cm) pile of £10 notes.
8,150	July price of a Metro Vanden Plas five-door car.
8,107	additional cost allowance paid to an MP for a constituency outside London.
8,100	purchasing power of the average Japanese.
8,068	annual wage of a boilermaker at Leyland Trucks.

8,049	annual wage of a track assembler at the Caterpillar Tractor Co Ltd.
8,000	value of 4.2 carat diamond which was swallowed by a man in an attempt to steal it. He was held while nature took its course.
8,000	ransom paid in September for two Labradors.
7,990	purchasing power of the average Finn.
7,944	annual wage of a carpenter at Metal Box.
7,874	annual cost of educating one state school pupil to five 0-level passes in Brent.
7,800	purchasing power of the average Dutchman.
7,750	price paid for the Lordship of the Manor of Walcot, Norfolk.
7,600	purchasing power of the average Briton.
7,595	July 1987 price of a Peugeot 205 1.6 auto five-door car.
7,540	annual wage of a capstan operator at Black Clawson International Ltd.
7,530	annual wage of an accounts clerk at the London Brick Co.
7,500	purchasing power of the average Austrian.
7,485	annual cost of educating one state school pupil to five 0-level passes in Wakefield.
7,433	salary of a Royal Navy midshipman after one year.
7,426	average annual wage of a buyer at GEC Telecommunications.
7,367	annual wage of a chauffeur at Talbot Motor Co.
7,289	July price of a Fiesta Ghia Auto 1.1 three-door car.

7,278	annual cost of educating one state school pupil to five 0-level passes in Manchester.
7,265	cost of buying a Polo mint for everyone living in Lancashire.
7,262	average annual wage of an assembler at Electrolux.
7,250	price paid for the Lordship of the Manor of Blewsbury, Berkshire.
7,250	quarterly turnover at which a business must register for VAT.
7,234	annual wage of a chargehand at Boots.
7,217	starting wage of a chargehand at GEC Telecommunications.
7,000	cost of buying a Mars bar for everyone living in Rutland.
7,000	average debt accumulated by an American student during his training.
6,999	July price of a Suzuki Swift GLXE 1.3 five-door car.
6,985	value of 5,500 lb (2,495 kg) of new pennies.
6,970	July price for Renault 5 Auto 1.4 five-door car.
6,915	July price of a Honda Civic 1.3 three-door car.
6,812	annual wage of a bricklayer at Perkins Engines.
6,750	July price of a Renault 5 Auto 1.4 three-door car.
6,734	July price of a Metro 1.3 auto three-door car.
6,714	cost of buying a Smartie for everyone living in Northern Ireland.
6,702	annual cost of educating one state school pupil to five 0-level passes in Wolverhampton.

6,700	price of 1 ton of fish oil.
6,660	value of a 1-cm-thick (0.39 in) pile of £20 notes.
6,659	July price of a Nissan Micra SGL 1.0 five-door car.
6,618	cost of buying a Smartie for everyone in Hampshire.
6,600	price paid in October for a ballet costume worn by Nijinsky.
6,600	purchasing power of the average Italian.
6,600	annual amount of capital gains before capital gains tax becomes payable.
6,583	annual cost of educating one state school pupil to five 0-level passes in Newcastle.
6,543	July price of a Ford Fiesta L Auto 1.1 three-door car.
6,500	compensation paid by a film director to each of Brigitte Bardot and Catherine Deneuve for revealing details of their private lives.
6,500	average earnings of a snail-breeder.
6,449	cost of buying a Smartie for everyone living in Essex.
6,432	July price of a Nissan Micra SGL 1.0 three-door car.
6,399	July price of Daihatsu Charade CX five-door car.
6,399	value of 134 lb (61 kg) of £1 coins.
6,380	July price of a Fiat Uno Selecta 1.1 five-door car.
6,353	value of a $1\frac{1}{2}$-in-thick (3.75 cm) pile of £5 notes.

6,340	annual wage of an accounts clerk at Cameron Iron Works.
6,331	total of the fine and costs imposed on the BBC for the death of Michael Lush while rehearsing a stunt for Noel Edmonds' show.
6,301	annual cost of educating one state school pupil to five 0-level passes in Liverpool.
6,300	cost of postage to send a first-class letter to everyone in Rutland.
6,250	award made by an American court to Charles Knapp against his mother for a broken ankle incurred while dancing.
6,188	cost of buying a Smartie for everyone living in Lesotho.
6,152	annual wage of a warehouseman at Tesco.
6,082	annual wage of a clerk at Albright and Wilson.
6,074	income below which a family with two children over 16 can claim family income supplement.
6,009	annual wages of a canteen worker at British Sugar.
6,000	inducement to accountants to work for Bromley Council.
5,980	starting salary of a Royal Navy midshipman.
5,980	minimum 'decent' annual wage, as defined by the Council of Europe.
5,964	income below which a family with two children aged between 11 and 16 can claim family income supplement.
5,939	average annual wage of a clerk at British Aerospace.
5,936	cost of buying a Polo mint for everyone in Botswana.

5,916	cost of buying a Smartie for everyone living in Lancashire.
5,897	July price of a Metro 1.3 City three-door car.
5,855	income below which a family with two children under the age of 11 can claim family income supplement.
5,841	annual cost of educating one state school pupil to five 0-level passes in Coventry.
5,701	annual cost of educating one state school pupil to five 0-level passes in Birmingham.
5,701	value of 2 tons of new pennies.
5,698	annual cost of educating one state school pupil to five 0-level passes in Nottinghamshire.
5,682	annual wage of a clerk at Westland Helicopters.
5,600	cost of buying a Mars bar for everyone living in Monaco.
5,555	average annual wage of a cashier at the Abbey National Building Society.
5,547	average annual wage of a cleaner for the Automobile Association.
5,501	price paid for a bottle of 1926 whisky.
5,500	average amount spent by a candidate in the 1987 general election.
5,480	cost of buying a Mars bar for everyone living in Liechtenstein.
5,412	average annual wage of a cashier at Makro.
5,390	compensation awarded to Michael Passmore for an explosion at work, as a result of which he lost interest in sex.
5,351	annual average wage of an assembler at Timex.

5,348	value of 1 cwt (50.8 kg) of £1 coins.
5,346	income below which a family with one child over 16 can claim family income supplement.
5,303	minimum annual wage of an assembler at Plessey.
5,302	annual wage of a barman at the BBC.
5,300	value of hash found in a baby's nappy in Spain in February.
5,291	income below which a family with one child aged between 11 and 16 can claim family income supplement.
5,258	cost of buying a Polo mint for everyone in Devon.
5,236	annual income below which a family with one child under 11 can claim family income supplement.
5,086	annual national average cost of educating one state school pupil to five 0-level passes.
5,080	value of a 6-in-high (15 cm) pile of £1 notes.
5,080	value of a line of £10 notes laid end to end from one end of a football pitch to the other.
5,043	annual wage of a head chef at a Thistle Hotel.
5,019	annual wage of a correspondence clerk at Littlewoods.
5,000	fine imposed on the editor of *The Sun* for contempt of court in reporting a murder case.
5,000	a 'portable discount' offered by Bromley Council to get people off its waiting list for council houses.
5,000	average cost of an artery bypass graft.
5,000	the average cost of a supervisor in bankruptcy (per Edgson-Wright).

5,000	value of 1 kg (2.2 lb) of 20p coins.
4,972	annual wage of a cashier at an Asda super-market.
4,960	annual cost of educating one state school pupil to five 0-level passes in Durham.
4,950	auction price for an 1850 golf ball.
4,931	annual cost of educating one state school pupil to five 0-level passes in Northamptonshire.
4,862	annual wage of a canteen worker at Granada Motorway Services.
4,840	annual amount charged to an overseas student studying science.
4,792	annual wage of a cleaner at Asda Stores.
4,785	annual cost of educating one state school pupil to five 0-level passes in Leicestershire.
4,761	annual wages of a canteen worker at Asda Stores.
4,750	July price of a Suzuki Alto 0.8 litre three-door car.
4,721	July price of a Mini 1000 Mayfair car.
4,702	annual cost of educating one state school pupil to five 0-level passes in Humberside.
4,700	purchasing power of the average Irishman.
4,697	average annual wage of a barman at Tennent Caledonian Breweries.
4,682	annual cost of educating one state school pupil to five 0-level passes in Norfolk.
4,675	amount a married pensioner is allowed to earn before he starts to pay income tax.
4,623	annual wages of an assistant butcher at Dew-hurst.

4,569	annual wages of a cleaner at the Co-op.
4,568	annual cost of educating one state school pupil to five O-level passes in Staffordshire.
4,550	annual wage of a cleaner at British Home Stores.
4,550	cost of postage to send a second-class letter to everyone in Rutland.
4,539	annual cost of educating one state school pupil to five O-level passes in Derbyshire.
4,500	fine imposed on Keith Best for illegal share applications.
4,492	value of half a ton of 10p pieces.
4,482	annual cost of educating one state school pupil to five O-level passes in Cumbria.
4,472	cost of buying a Mars bar for everyone living in San Marino.
4,462	annual cost of educating one state school pupil to five O-level passes on the Isle of Wight.
4,413	annual cost of educating one state school pupil to five O-level passes in Bedfordshire.
4,335	cost of buying a Smartie for everyone living in Surrey.
4,331	costs payable by the BBC to the inquiry into the death of Michael Lush while rehearsing for Noel Edmonds' show.
4,320	cost of buying a Mars bar for everyone living in the Cayman Islands.
4,316	cost of buying a Smartie for everyone living in Birmingham.
4,281	cost of buying a Smartie for everyone living in Devon.
4,235	value of a 1-in-thick (2.5 cm) pile of £5 notes.

4,209	annual cost of educating one state school pupil to five 0-level passes in Lancashire.
4,162	annual cost of educating one state school pupil to five 0-level passes in Devon.
4,064	value of 2 cwt (101.6 kg) of 20p coins.
4,060	average purchasing power of a Greek.
4,024	annual cost of educating one state school pupil to five 0-level passes in Essex.
4,000	value of tools stolen by thieves from a gear box repair company in Axford, Wiltshire, in April, with which they then burgled the local post office.
4,000	UK imports from Kiribati.
4,000	fine imposed on the Marquess of Hertford for ploughing a Roman site on his land.
3,989	annual cost of educating one state school pupil to five 0-level passes in Wiltshire.
3,954	July price of a Mini 1000 City car.
3,954	annual cost of educating one state school pupil to five 0-level passes in Cheshire.
3,947	street value of 1 oz (28.35 g) of heroin.
3,908	annual cost of educating one state school pupil to five 0-level passes in Berkshire.
3,853	cost of buying a Mars bar for everyone living in the Orkney Islands.
3,852	annual cost of educating one state school pupil to five 0-level passes in Hampshire.
3,830	cost of buying a Polo mint for everyone in Norfolk.
3,795	amount which a married man can earn before he starts to pay income tax.

3,715	annual cost of educating one state school pupil to five 0–level passes in Cambridgeshire.
3,709	annual cost of educating one state school pupil to five 0–level passes in Oxfordshire.
3,700	cost of a traditional wedding (per *Wedding and Home* magazine).
3,690	annual charge to an overseas student for studying an arts course.
3,683	annual cost of educating one state school pupil to five 0–level passes in Warwickshire.
3,670	purchasing power of the average Portuguese.
3,600	annual cost of educating one state school pupil to five 0–level passes in Hertfordshire.
3,593	value of 4 tons of 10p coins.
3,582	annual cost of educating one state school pupil to five 0–level passes in East Sussex.
3,542	cost of buying a Polo mint for everyone in Cyprus.
3,500	price of the first juke box designed to play compact discs.
3,500	price paid to an umpire for a centre court ticket at Wimbledon. The umpire resigned.
3,500	maximum payable under the Athens Convention for a child drowned on a ferry.
3,492	grant for a London postgraduate student.
3,469	price paid for 10 drawings by John Profumo. They were bought for £5,000 in 1963.
3,454	annual cost of educating one state school pupil to five 0–level passes in Kent.
3,422	annual cost of educating one state school pupil to five 0–level passes in Buckinghamshire.
3,405	price of 1 ton of mint imperials.

3,405	cost of buying a Polo mint for everyone in Swaziland.
3,370	maximum amount a candidate could spend in the general election, plus an allowance per voter.
3,354	annual income from a 100% industrial disablement benefit.
3,345	cost to an employment rehabilitation centre of resettling one disabled person.
3,330	value of 1-cm-high (0.39 in) pile of £10 notes.
3,315	price of 1 ton of Nuttalls Mintoes.
3,322	annual cost of educating one state school pupil to five 0-level passes in Dorset.
3,300	cost of a hip replacement operation.
3,263	cost of the National Health Service per person.
3,229	annual cost of educating one state school pupil to five 0-level passes in North Yorkshire.
3,200	compensation awarded by the European Court to John Townend, and his father, for a caning received while John was a pupil.
3,164	annual cost of educating one state school pupil to five 0-level passes in Surrey.
3,136	price of 1 ton of Liquorice Allsorts.
3,119	cost of buying a Smartie for everyone living in Norfolk.
3,046	price of 1 ton of Turkish delight.
3,000	reported price for a newborn baby in Cosenza, Italy.
3,000	annual chattels exemption for capital gains tax.

L

2,985	annual cost of educating one state school pupil to five 0-level passes in West Sussex (cheapest in UK).
2,960	amount which a single pensioner is allowed to earn before he starts to pay income tax.
2,957	price of 1 ton of Dolly Mixtures.
2,920	professional indemnity insurance premium for a solicitor earning £100,000 a year.
2,859	grant for a postgraduate student living outside London.
2,851	value of 1 ton of new pennies.
2,800	value of the UK national debt per person.
2,773	cost of buying a Smartie for everyone living in Swaziland.
2,754	cost of buying a Polo mint for everyone in Bedfordshire.
2,688	price of 1 ton of fudge.
2,584	price of 1 ton of chocolate.
2,500	fine imposed on Channel 4 on 14 April for its programme *Irish Angle*, accused of prejudicing a trial.
2,498	value of 1.5-cm-thick (0.59 in) pile of £5 notes.
2,425	amount of income which may be earned tax-free by a single person.
2,400	maximum amount which may be invested in a personal equity plan.
2,400	annual retainer allegedly paid to John Browne MP to lobby for a Lebanese firm.
2,392	cost of buying a Smartie for everyone living in Cleveland.
2,330	grant for a London undergraduate.

2,300	extra tax assessment if you have a company car less than four years old which cost more than £29,000.
2,242	cost of buying a Smartie for everyone living in Bedfordshire.
2,075	grant for a postgraduate student who lives at home.
2,054	annual value of the married man's old age pension.
2,054	cost of buying a Polo mint for everyone in Shropshire.
2,032	value of 1 cwt (50.8 kg) of 20p coins.
2,011	value of a line of £1 coins placed edge to edge from one end of a football pitch to the other.
2,000	fine imposed on the BBC for ignoring safety standards, which led to the death of Michael Lush while rehearsing a stunt for Noel Edmonds' TV programme.
2,000	amount raised by St Michael's and All Angels, Bedford Park, for charity, by singing all 542 hymns in the *English Hymnal*.
2,000	cost of a 'Lesbian Day' organised by Camden Council.
2,000	minimum balance needed to keep a bank account at Coutts.
1,972	grant for an undergraduate student living outside London.
1,960	amount lost by a pensionable married couple since the earnings-related supplement was abolished in 1980.
1,953	cost of buying a Smartie for everyone living in Somerset.
1,922	part of student grant payable by parents earning £19,000.

L

1,912	cost of buying a Smartie for everyone living in Cornwall.
1,882	value of 1 cwt (50.8 kg) of 50p coins.
1,730	postgraduate fee payable by EEC students.
1,714	cost of buying a Smartie for everyone living in Bristol.
1,672	cost of buying a Smartie for everyone living in Shropshire.
1,672	part of student grant payable by parents earning £18,000.
1,665	value of a 1-cm-thick (0.39 in) pile of £5 notes.
1,631	price of 1 ton of coffee on the commodity market in January.
1,620	professional indemnity insurance premium for a solicitor earning £50,000 a year.
1,569	grant to an undergraduate student who lives at home.
1,530	extra tax assessment if you have a company car which is more than four years old and originally cost more than £29,000.
1,450	price paid for a 12-year-old bottle of whisky signed by Mrs Thatcher. (One signed by Neil Kinnock raised £25.)
1,450	fine imposed on Harvey Proctor for gross indecency.
1,450	extra tax assessment if you have a company car under four years old which originally cost between £19,250 and £29,000.
1,437	part of a student grant payable by parents earning £17,000.
1,407	maximum national insurance payable by one person.

1,401	price of 1 ton of ice cream.
1,370	additional amount a single parent is allowed to earn before starting to pay income tax.
1,350	amount spent by the Inner London Education Authority in buying GLC silver.
1,344	threatened fine on USA TV commentator David Brinkley for 10 cents' arrears of tax to the District of Colombia.
1,300	projected price of a DAT tape-playing machine by Sony.
1,255	amount spent by Inner London Education Authority educating one primary school pupil (highest in the country).
1,249	amount lost by a single pensioner as a result of abolishing the earnings-related supplement in 1980.
1,237	part of a student grant payable by parents earning £16,000.
1,235	annual value of a single person's old age pension.
1,230	price of 1 ton of coffee on the commodity market in April (five-year low).
1,191	cost of buying a Smartie for everyone living in Nottingham.
1,170	weekly cost to Merton Council of keeping a child under 17 in a secure unit.
1,155	annual amount spent by Haringey Council in educating a primary school pupil.
1,100	extra tax assessment if you have a company car up to four years old with an engine capacity above 2,000 cc.
1,086	cost of buying a Smartie for everyone living in Plymouth.

135

£

1,084	cost of buying a Smartie for everyone living in Barbados.
1,080	annual insurance premium paid by a family doctor to cover him for negligence claims.
1,080	additional tax relief given to a blind couple.
1,069	cost of buying a Smartie for everyone living in Stoke-on-Trent.
1,068	value of a line of 20p coins placed edge to edge from one end of a football pitch to the other.
1,065	cost of buying a Polo mint for everyone living in Southampton.
1,037	part of a student grant payable by parents earning £15,000.
1,000	bill for damages presented by the White Horse to Abingdon Round Table for damage caused at a rowdy meeting.
1,000	UK imports from Equitorial Guinea.
1,000	amount paid by Ebbw Vale Council to move the chairman's seat by 9 in (22.5 cm) so that other councillors could get past.
987	average tax charged in the EEC on a 38-ton lorry.
970	extra tax assessment if you have a company car which originally cost between £19,250 and £29,000 and is less than four years old.
960	licence for a jackpot gaming machine which takes 10p and higher value coins.
950	cost of *The Encyclopedia of Religion* in nine volumes, published by Macmillan.
950	cost of removing an eye cataract.
923	cost of buying a Smartie for everyone living in Derby.

915	maximum amount of Class 4 national insurance payable.
900	maximum annual charge for a security box at Knightsbridge Safe Deposit Centre (robbed in July).
900	value of a line of £10 notes placed end to end down a cricket pitch.
865	cost of buying a Polo mint for everyone in Milton Keynes.
850	price of 1 ton of aluminium.
837	part of student grant payable by parents earning £14,000.
836	cost of buying a Polo mint for everyone in Basildon.
768	amount Wandsworth Council spends on renovation per council house.
750	fine imposed on comedian Adrian Edmondson in April for drinking and driving.
725	extra tax assessment if you have a company car, four or more years old, with an engine capacity above 2000 cc.
711	cost of buying a Smartie for everyone living in Luton.
704	cost of buying a Smartie for everyone living in Milton Keynes.
700	normal nightly rate for the Presidential Suite in the Ramada Hotel where Neil Kinnock stayed during the Labour Party conference.
700	extra tax assessment if you have a company car up to four years old with an engine between 1401 and 2000 cc.
690	Robert Maxwell's daily hotel bill during the Labour Party conference.

683	amount left in the will of the fourth Baron Hothfield.
681	cost of buying a Smartie for everyone living in Basildon.
655	annual amount spent by Somerset Council per primary pupil (lowest in the country).
637	part of student grant payable by parents earning £13,000.
634	cost of buying a Smartie for everyone living in Motherwell.
625	cost of buying a Smartie for everyone living in Blackpool.
624	Belgian road tax for a 38-ton lorry.
600	fine imposed by Football Association on Mark Dennis for comments he made about Southampton manager Chris Nicholl.
600	average cost of rewiring a house when done by direct labour organisation of a London Borough, according to a report done.
600	amount which a lady left in her will to Cardiff social security benefit office for their 'care and consideration'.
598	annual farming subsidy per family.
556	undergraduate fee charged to an EEC student.
551	cost of buying a Polo mint for everyone living in Stratford-on-Avon.
545	weekly cost paid by Brent Council to keep James Joyce, an unemployed Irishman, and his family at Kensington International Hotel.
540	additional tax relief given to a blind taxpayer.
537	cost of buying a Smartie for everyone living in Guildford.

532	cost of buying a Smartie for everyone living on the Isle of Wight.
525	extra tax assessment for a company car up to four years old with an engine up to 1,400 cc.
500	price paid for a bottle of whisky signed by Clint Eastwood.
500	cost of buying a Smartie for everyone living in Chester.
500	fine imposed on footballer Mo Johnston for assaulting a hairdresser.
500	limit on small claims procedure at the County Court.
500	amount paid by Hillingdon Council to fly Conservative Councillor Jonathan Bianco back from holiday in Tenerife for a vote on council spending.
500	compensation paid by the TSB to a housewife after wrongly telling a store to tear up her credit card.
500	limit on a cheque card by using Cheque Point Guarantee.
500	minimum fee for joining FIMBRA.
500	prize money for thinking of a name for the ethical trust promoted by N. M. Schroder.
499	price (excluding VAT) for an Amstrad PCW 9512 word processor with a daisy wheel printer.
498	cost of buying a Smartie for everyone living in Oxford.
490	cost of buying a Smartie for everyone living in Canterbury.
490	average amount donated to charity by an American family.

484	amount of the unpaid gambling debt which had multi-millionaire Jeffrey Archer banned from all racecourses.
470	extra tax assessment if you have a company car four or more years old, with an engine capacity between 1,400 and 2,000 cc.
456	average amount spent each year on furniture by childless couples in the 25–34 age range.
456	average solicitor's fee for purchasing a £100,000 house.
450	premium for gazumping insurance offered by Abbey National.
449	value of 1 cwt (50.8 kg) of 10p coins.
448	cost of buying a Smartie for everyone living in Stratford–upon–Avon.
439	cost of buying a Smartie for everyone living in York.
401	value of a line of 10p coins placed edge to edge from one end of a football pitch to the other.
397	part of a student grant payable by parents earning £11,800.
390	cost of buying a Smartie for everyone living in Gloucester.
375	licence for an amusement–with–prizes gaming machine which takes 10p or higher value coins.
372	cost of buying a Smartie for everyone living in Durham.
355	value of £1 coins placed edge to edge down a cricket pitch.
352	average annual amount spent on providing care for a Scotsman (highest region in the UK).

350	daily fee for the hospital where Anne Diamond had her baby.
350	price of the 1-oz (28.35 g) gold Britannia coin.
350	extra tax assessment if you have a company car, four or more years old, with an engine capacity of less than 1,400 cc.
346	monthly payment on a repayment mortgage for £40,000, over 25 years.
342	cost of buying a Polo mint for everyone living in the Seychelles.
340	fine on footballer Alan Sunderland for drinking and driving.
337	average solicitor's fee for conveyance of a house costing between £45,000 and £75,000.
323	monthly repayment on an endowment mortgage for £40,000 over 25 years.
322	average amount donated to charity by a British family.
319	cost of buying a Smartie for everyone living in Stevenage.
309	average pension paid per head of population in Greater London (highest for any part of the country).
300	cost of installing one of the new types of stamp-vending machines.
300	fine imposed on two girls who ran a brothel, using government funds, under the Enterprise Allowance scheme.
300	fine imposed on comedian Jim Davidson for drinking and driving.
300	fine imposed on Sir Charles Kerruish, speaker in the Manx parliament, for contravention of sheep movement regulations.

300	minimum price of a dress by Norman Hartnell.
299	reduced price (excluding VAT) of the PCW 8256 word processor when the newer model was brought out.
295	average amount spent by a bride on a wedding dress, veil and shoes.
295	cost of a Liberty crown from Pobjoy mint, legal tender in the Isle of Man.
285	average amount spent each year on furniture by someone aged between 25 and 44 and in the AB social group.
282	part of student grant payable by parents with an income of £11,000.
281	price of a krugerrand.
280	fine imposed by Oxford magistrates on Prince Watid Bin Saad, nephew of King Fahad of Saudi Arabia, for possessing cocaine and cannabis.
280	price of 1 oz (28.35 g) of gold (October).
280	price of a sun recorder.
279	cost of buying a Smartie for everyone living in the Seychelles.
278	price of 1 oz (28.35 g) of gold (April).
274	average rent arrears per council house tenant in Greater London.
260	cost of buying a Smartie for everyone living in Inverness.
256	average solicitor's fee for buying a house.
255	average weekly earnings for a man living in Greater London.
250	monthly payment under a repayment mortgage for £30,000 over 25 years.

250	price of the newly launched pocket colour television set.
250	fine imposed on snooker player Alex Hurricane Higgins for head-butting an official.
243	average amount spent on an engagement ring.
242	value of 5p coins placed edge to edge down a football pitch
233	average amount spent on providing care for someone in Oxfordshire (lowest region in the UK).
233	average weekly earnings of a man in south-east England (April 1986).
230	price of Clive Sinclair's Z88 portable computer.
219	monthly payment for an endowment mortgage of £30,000 over 25 years.
217	cost of buying a Smartie for everyone living in Corby.
206	average amount someone in the south east spends each year on furniture.
204	weekly cost of social security per person in Northern Ireland (highest area in UK).
202	average amount Lambeth Council spends each year renovating each council house.
202	monthly earnings from which the PAYE tax system must be operated.
200	going rate for a 'classic' Levi jacket with original yellow stitching, rather than the modern orange stitching.
200	fee to 'adopt' a book at the British Library.
200	fine imposed on Lord Blandford on 2 April for speeding

200	reward given to Philip Stubbs, who found £75,000 worth of jewels and other valuables in a hedge.
200	court fee for the voluntary winding up of a limited company.
200	amount for which Camden Council sold each of its street lights in a leaseback deal to beat government spending limits.
195.00	price of 10 pa'anga coin from Tonga, containing 1 oz (28.35 g) of platinum.
194.90	excise duty charged on 1 hectolitre (22 gal) of wine with an alcoholic strength above 22%.
190.00	price of 10 pa'anga coin from Tonga containing 10 oz (283.5 g) of silver.
188.00	value of 20p coins placed edge to edge down a cricket pitch.
184.20	cost of buying a Polo mint for everyone in Rutland.
183.04	monthly payment for an endowment mortgage of £25,000 over 25 years.
182.00	average weekly earnings by a man in Northern Ireland (April 1986).
173.00	capital expenditure on universities per student.
172.50	cost of a one-day session at the Café Royal for members of the Labour Party.
170.24	price of 1 cwt (50.8 kg) of mint imperials.
169.00	average weekly earnings by a woman in Greater London (April 1986).
169.00	monthly earnings at which national insurance becomes payable.
169.00	excise duty charged on 1 hectolitre (22 gal) of

wine with an alcoholic strength of between 15 and 22%.

166.75   monthly payment for a repayment mortgage of £20,000 over 25 years.

165.76   price of 1 cwt (50.8 kg) of Nuttalls Mintoes.

162.00   hourly rate charged by one plumber during the cold spell in January.

160.00   average home's quarterly gas bill.

160.00   cost of the amount of stock which goes missing each week from Tip Top Drugstores.

156.80   price of 1 cwt (50.8 kg) of Liquorice Allsorts.

156.00   average amount a Scotsman spends each year on furniture.

154.00   average wages of a woman in south-east England (April 1986).

152.32   price of 1 cwt (50.8 kg) of Turkish delight.

151.00   average fee for a wedding photographer.

150.00   cost of buying a Smartie for everyone living in Rutland.

150.00   licence for a gaming machine which pays prizes up to £4 and which is operated by a 2p or 5p coin.

147.84   price of 1 cwt (50.8 kg) of Dolly Mixtures.

146.43   monthly payment of an endowment mortgage of £20,000 over 25 years.

145.00   cost of one night at the Ritz.

145.00   additional tax relief which a married woman may claim for looking after a dependent relative.

142.54   value of 1 cwt (50.8 kg) of new pennies.

140.00   part of student grant payable by parents earning £10,000.

145

134.40	price of 1 cwt (50.8 kg) of fudge.
125.05	monthly payment of a repayment mortgage of £15,000 over 25 years.
125.00	fine imposed on Cecil Parkinson's daughter for drug offences.
125.00	amount for which Camden Council sold each of its parking meters in a leaseback deal designed to negate the government's spending limits on local authorities.
123.00	minimum weekly wage introduced at Lambeth Council.
121.00	cost of buying a Mars bar for everyone living on Sark.
115.00	'decency threshold' for weekly wages, per Council of Europe.
115.00	maximum fee for dental treatment.
113.00	cost of buying a Smartie for everyone living in Berwick-upon-Tweed.
109.82	monthly payment of an endowment mortgage of £15,000 over 25 years.
107.00	donation from prisoners at Pentonville to victims of the Zeebrugge ferry disaster.
105.00	amount allegedly paid to human volunteers to test antidotes to nerve gas.
100.00	nominal value of a 1-oz (28.35 g) Britannia gold coin.
100.00	fine imposed on Viscount Linley for speeding.
100.00	fine imposed on PC Frederick Connah for calling an inspector 'flower'.
100.00	additional tax relief which a person (other than a married woman) may claim for looking after a dependent relative.

100.00	cost of the grant of a betting agency permit.
98.00	excise duty on 1 hectolitre (22 gal) of wine with a strength of up to 15%.
91.70	value of 1p invested at 5% in 1800.
90.00	amount stolen, for which Joseph Cleaver and four others were burnt alive at Fordingbridge.
88.20	value of 2p coins placed edge to edge down a football pitch.
82.57	cost of buying a Smartie for everyone living in the Scilly Isles.
80.00	gadget sold as a security device to make a woman's voice sound like a man's on the telephone.
80.00	spot price for 1 oz (28.35 g) of platinum (March).
80.00	cost of a betting office licence.
75.00	price of a UK-made top quality cricket bat.
75.00	the consultancy fee which would have shown that the safety harness, fatally used by Michael Lush rehearsing a stunt for Noel Edmonds' BBC show, was unsafe
75.00	price of a DIY coffin kit sold in New Zealand.
75.00	estimated cost of each oral answer given to a parliamentary question.
70.60	value of 10p coins placed edge to edge down a cricket pitch.
70.05	price of 1 cwt (50.8 kg) of ice cream.
70.00	amount Jeffrey Archer was (falsely) alleged to have paid Monica Coghlan for a night's sex.
67.00	price of an imported top quality cricket bat.
65.00	fine paid by Lord Carrington on 12 June for dangerous driving.

65.00	amount stolen from a petrol station at Kennford near Exeter by a man dressed as a clown.
65.00	fine imposed on Linda Bellos, leader of Lambeth Council, for not taxing her car.
63.11	average daily rate charged by a London hotel.
63.00	average rent arrears owed by a council house tenant.
61.84	cost of buying a Smartie for everyone living in Bournemouth.
61.08	cost of BUPA cover for a 34–year-old couple living in London.
58.13	rent per square foot for office space in the City of London (May).
58.00	cost of a colour television licence.
57.00	fee payable to get your car out of a London car pound.
56.23	value of new pennies placed edge to edge down a football pitch.
55.00	cost per head of finding people a job by the Manpower Services Commission.
55.00	additional tax relief for a taxpayer who relies on the services of his son or daughter.
54.00	part of student grant payable by parents earning £9,400.
53.00	daily increase in the value of a home in London.
51.99	price of a telephone from Mercury Communications.
50.00	price paid for a human skull in a pub in Lichfield. The seller was charged with grave-robbing.
50.00	price asked for in a newspaper advertisement

for a set of clockwork clowns. The telephone number was that of Colchester United Football Club.

50.00 price paid for each council house on Penywaun estate in South Wales.

50.00 amount paid for each of 83 council houses sold by Cynon Valley District Council to property developers.

50.00 daily allowance to competitors in the Wimbledon lawn tennis championship.

50.00 fine imposed on Ian Willis for selling *Spycatcher* outside Harrods.

50.00 maximum amount guaranteed by a cheque card.

50.00 reward for finding a stolen cheque card.

49.64 excise duty charged on 1 kg (2.2 lb) of hand-rolling tobacco.

47.20 weekly statutory sick pay rate for someone whose normal weekly earnings are over £76.49.

47.05 excise duty charged on 1 kg (2.2 lb) of cigars.

46.50 weekly earnings at which income tax becomes payable under the PAYE scheme.

46.34 average amount spend on educating a secondary school pupil.

45.00 amount paid for a second-hand computer, bought at an army surplus store, which contained the Ministry of Defence's RSRE secret program.

45.00 estimated cost of each written answer given to a parliamentary question.

42.65 value of 5p coins placed edge to edge down a cricket pitch.

41.15	monthly BUPA premium for health cover for a young family of four.
40.27	average amount provided by a local authority to educate one secondary school pupil.
40.00	weekly payment under the Enterprise Allowance scheme.
40.00	price paid for a bottle of whisky signed by Dame Edna Everidge.
40.00	monthly cost of a cellular telephone.
39.50	weekly old–age pension for a married man.
39.05	average daily rate charged by a British hotel.
39.00	weekly earnings at which national insurance becomes payable.
35.00	price of a bottle of premium Scotch in Japan.
35.00	cost of an annual 'season ticket' for prescription charges.
34.56	average daily rate charged by a Scottish hotel.
32.85	statutory sick pay rate for someone who normally earns between £39.01 and £47.20 a week.
31.60	weekly attendance allowance for someone who needs attention day and night.
31.00	average cost of one hour of an accountant's time (two- or three-man practice based in London).
30.00	price paid for bottles of whisky signed by Norman Tebbit or David Owen.
30.00	fee paid to wrestler 'King Kong' for the bout in which he died.
30.00	amount of the death grant prior to its abolition in 1987.

29.93	average amount spent per year on a primary school pupil.
29.80	monthly BUPA premium for a 26-year-old living in London.
27.00	weekly grant payable to sixthformers under proposals advanced by the Labour Party.
26.00	average cost of one hour of an accountant's time (sole practitioner based in London).
25.80	excise duty charged on 1 hectolitre (22 gal) of beer.
25.00	fine imposed on John Farmer at Newton Abbot on 25 June for assaulting a primrose (a protected species).
25.00	price paid for a bottle of whisky signed by Neil Kinnock.
25.00	fine imposed on Peter Robinson MP for not taxing his car. He chose to spend seven days in jail instead.
24.95	excise duty on 1 kg (2.2 lb) of tobacco other than in the form of cigars, cigarettes or hand-rolling tobacco.
23.75	weekly rate for the severe disablement allowance.
22.78	cost of a 10-minute call to New York from a Park Lane hotel. (British Telecom's charge is £5.89.)
22.00	minimum share-dealing charge at Debenhams.
21.10	weekly attendance allowance for someone who needs attention during the day only, or during the night only.
21.00	assets of Sampat Sethia when he was declared bankrupt for liabilities of £20 million.

20.00	price paid for a bottle of whisky signed by Tony Benn.
20.00	value of a new postal order which was introduced.
20.00	attendance fee at the House of Lords.
20.00	bonus paid by the Co-op to undertaking staff for every extra funeral they obtain.
19.38	excise duty charged on 1 litre (0.22 gal) of light oil.
18.04	average amount per primary school pupil paid by a local authority.
18.00	price per bottle at which 1986 claret was put on the market.
18.00	cost of a black and white television licence.
17.00	price of a normal bottle of Scotch in Japan.
16.39	excise duty charged on 1 litre (0.22 gal) of derv.
16.00	minimum charge for the Barclayshare Investor Account Service.
15.80	excise duty on 1 hectolitre (22 gal) of cider.
15.77	excise duty on 1 litre (0.22 gal) of spirits.
15.52	value of 2p coins placed edge to edge down a cricket pitch.
15.00	price paid for a bottle of whisky signed by Roy Hattersley.
15.00	charge for renewing a betting office licence.
13.00	price of a copy of *Household Food Consumption and Expenditure 1985*.
12.52	price of an MOT for a car from 3 August.
12.50	cost of a four-month 'season ticket' for prescription charges.

12.00	charge for a bookmaker's permit or a betting agency permit.
11.95	copy of *Roget's Thesaurus*, latest edition published 15 June.
11.89	average amount per primary school pupil provided by parents and other non-local authority sources.
11.50	average weekly farm subsidy per family.
10.92	average annual amount spend on books per secondary school pupil.
10.45	quarterly fee for British Telecom's Total Care service, guaranteeing a four-hour response around the clock.
10.20	copy of the Finance Bill 1987.
10.00	fine imposed on hearses turning up 15 minutes late in Birmingham.
10.00	Christmas bonus paid to pensioners and other recipients of certain social security benefits.
10.00	monthly fee for a Vector bank account at Midland Bank.
9.90	value of new pennies placed edge to edge down a cricket pitch.
8.99	price of a compact disc of newly recorded music.
8.75	marketing cost for each British Gas share application. The cost was criticised by the National Audit Office.
8.62	cost of Mercury telephone authorisation code.
8.60	copy of the Finance Act 1987.
8.50	copy of Debtors (Scotland) Act 1987.
8.36	cost of buying a Smartie for everyone living in the Shetlands.

8.00	annual subscription for hiring an art treasure from Manchester City Art Gallery.
7.90	copy of the Finance (No 2) Act 1987.
7.70	copy of the Bill which became the Finance (No 2) Act 1987.
7.48	price of an MOT for a motorcycle from 3 August.
7.51	average annual amount spent on books per primary school pupil.
7.25	weekly child benefit.
7.00	office rent per square foot (0.0929 sq m) in Leeds (January).
6.80	price of the annual report by the Director of Fair Trading.
6.50	National Health Service spending per person per week.
6.20	average weekly donation to charity by a British family.
6.07	average parental donation to complement annual state spending on a secondary school pupil.
5.95	copy of *The Writers and Artists Yearbook* 1987.
5.55	the average cost of making up a prescription.
5.30	copy of the Family Law Reform Act 1987.
5.30	copy of the Consumer Protection Act 1987.
5.00	the going rate for making a fraudulent share application.
5.00	cold weather payment made to social security recipients when the temperature fell below zero.
4.90	cost of a breakfast promoted by the Man-

power Services Commission to promote its schemes.

4.00 spot price for 1 oz (28.35 g) of silver (March).

3.95 weekly rate for the voluntary (Class 3) national insurance.

3.80 quarterly charge for Prompt Care, the British Telecom service which guarantees a four-hour response during working hours.

3.50 copy of *Making Money on the Stock Exchange – after the crash*, a terrific book by the same author as this one (same publishers too!)

3.30 copy of the Criminal Justice Act 1987.

3.30 offer price of a BP share.

2.87 value of a BP share when sold by the UK government for £3.30.

2.45 issue price of a share in British Airports Authority.

2.40 prescription charge.

2.14 price of 1 oz (28.35 g) of Golden Virginia Tobacco.

2.05 price of a share in Sock Shop when it started trading in May. The offer price was £1.25.

2.00 amount which Richard Tibbo paid an 11-year-old and a 13-year-old girl for a strip-tease show.

2.00 approximate price requested for each item of Concorde china sold off when British Airways changed its livery.

2.00 cost of making a compact disc.

1.54 price of 20 Embassy No 1 King Size cigarettes.

1.50 price charged by some grocers for a loaf of bread during the January freeze.

1.40	1 lb (0.45 kg) of barley sugar.
1.39	value of a £1 TSB share when the third instalment was payable.
1.27	amount universities were able to raise in 1985/86 from independent sources for each £1 provided by the government. The figure for 1982 was £2.67.
1.25	issue price of a share in the Sock Shop.
1.20	price of 1 lb (0.45 kg) of humbugs.
1.20	cost of laundering a shirt collar.
1.15	excise duty charged on a 'short standard' of matches (i.e. 7,200 matches).
1.00	offer in *Private Eye* classified ads for finding out how to raise easy money (answer: place more ads like this one).
1.00	entrance fee for a performance of Handel's *Messiah* at St Chad's, Shrewsbury to raise funds for the Liberal Party.
1.00	daily fine payable by a stockbroker for not settling an account outstanding from October 1986.
1.00	admission fee to the RAF Museum.
90p	price of the new legal magazine *Lawyer*.
89p	price of a 200 gm (7 oz) bar of milk chocolate.
85p	issue price of a partly paid share in Rolls-Royce.
70p	value of 1p invested at 5% in 1900.
60p	price of $\frac{1}{2}$ lb (227 g) of humbugs.
55p	charge made by Barclays Bank for processing a cheque.
55p	price of new satirical magazine *Digger*.

50p the going rate for a condom, sold as a water bomb, after the Health Boards community medicine service in Aberdeen let 12- and 13-year-old children have them three dozen at a time.

50p charge made by Lloyds Bank for processing a cheque.

50p excise duty charged on a cigarette lighter.

46.9p mileage allowance paid to MPs.

45p third instalment payable on a British Gas share in June.

43p price of an 11 oz (312 g) pack of ice cream.

43p value of a 50p unit in the Royal Life unit trust two weeks after its launch.

40p balance on a Sears charge card for which Rosemary McRobert, director of the Consumer's Association, was charged £29.95 interest and threatened with blacklisting.

40p price of *The Financial Times*.

38p price of 4 oz (113 g) of mint imperials.

38p charge for one minute on British Telecom's talkabout line.

37 $\frac{1}{2}$ p share price of Pavion International, cosmetic makers, on 14 August 1987. The company took the most unusual step of saying this share price was not justified.

37p price of 4 oz (113 g) of Nuttalls Mintoes.

37p cost of a dog licence.

35p price of *News on Sunday* launched in April.

35p price of 4 oz (113 g) of barley sugar.

35p price of 4 oz (113 g) of Liquorice Allsorts.

33p price of 4 oz (113 g) of Dolly Mixtures.

32p	price of a 2-oz (58 g) packet of Victory V lozenges.
31p	cost of sending a letter to America.
30p	price of 4 oz (113 g) of fudge.
29p	price of 4 oz (113 g) of liquorice comfits.
26p	price of a pint of milk.
20p	price of a Mars bar.
20p	fare charged by Gloucester Bus Company for a 3-ft high teddy bear (the charge was subsequently refunded).
20p	price of a packet of Trebor mints.
18p	amount stolen by a thief from a woman's handbag in Nairobi in June. A mob burnt him alive.
18p	cost of sending a first-class letter up to 60 gm.
14p	price of a packet of crisps.
13p	cost of sending a second-class letter up to 60 gm.
12p	price of a Mates condom.
10p	price of *London Daily News* while it was competing against *Evening Standard* and *Evening News*.
10p	cost to British Telecom of processing a direct debit.
10p	amount at dispute in a dominoes game which led to William Smith being bitten in the nose and requiring surgery.
8p	value of 1p invested at 5% in 1945.
8p	amount which students at Mansfield College, Oxford said they were being overcharged daily on student rents and against which they went on a rent strike.

6p	dividend on a Britoil share.
5p	price of *Evening News* while it was competing against *London Daily News*.
3.4p	administration cost from each £1 collected by Christian Aid.
$\frac{1}{2}$**p**	price of a sheet of A4 paper.
nothing	fee paid to Faye Dunaway for acting in the film *Barfly*.
nothing	compensation to 11-year-old Marlon Baker who suffered serious mental illness caused by a wrong diagnosis.
nothing	total rates paid by the village of Knighton, Staffordshire. They were granted an exemption in 1660.